The
Disciplined
Investor

Essential Strategies for Success

The
Disciplined
Investor

Essential Strategies for Success

Andrew Horowitz, CFP

Second Edition

HFactor Publishing

Published by HFactor Publishing
1555 NorthPark Drive, Suite 102, Weston, Florida 33326
info@thedisciplinedinvestor.com
or visit www.thedisciplinedinvestor.com

The Disciplined Investor: Essential Strategies for Success
Andrew Horowitz, CFP

Library of Congress Cataloging-in-Publication Data
Horowitz, Andrew.
    The disciplined investor: essential strategies for success / Andrew
    Horowitz.—2nd ed.
    p. cm.

ISBN 10: 0-9787083-7-7
ISBN 13: 978-0-9787083-7-5
1. Title 2. Author 3. Personal Finance/Investments
Library of Congress Control Number: 2007939925

Printed in the United States of America
10 9 8 7 6 5 4 3 2

Acknowledgements and Dedication

The process of writing a book is not an easy one. There are countless hours that need to be dedicated, all requiring focus without distraction. To help me, I had input from many individuals. They have all helped to bring *The Disciplined Investor* from its idea stage in early 1999 to the final written and bound product. A big thank you is due to all that have come together in an amazing show of support.

Time, proofreading, and research are just a few of the essential tools that this special group of family, friends, and colleagues provided. All of these are integral parts of the process that helped me achieve the finished product.

The first and foremost person that I would like to acknowledge is my wife, Jill, for her dedication to me and our family. Without her, I would wander aimlessly day by day. She is my north-star and my best friend, now and always.

My children, Lauren, Erica, and Brett will be the first to get copies of the final print. They are my biggest fans, and I am theirs. Each of them has a way of making me feel personally and professionally successful from the moment they wake to the time they go to sleep. Just looking at them fills me with overwhelming pride when I think of the fine people they have become.

Marnie Goldberg is my right hand as well as my left. She is my Radar O'Reilly; she seems to know what I am thinking, even before I do. As an Assistant, there is none better. As a friend she has no competition. She is a rare jewel that I hope will be a part of my personal and professional life for a very long time.

Dedication, creativity, and organization are the hallmarks of anyone who is successful. That clearly defines Michelle McMillan, who has helped to organize this book from the pre-proof stage. Michelle has an amazingly positive attitude and brings a fresh edge to her work. All in all, she is the kind of person that has your back and helps to bring calm to the everyday chaos.

A special thank you goes out to many of the people who helped bring information and research to the meetings when I first began planning the contents for this book. One particular person who had a hand in the process and should be recognized for his hard work is Kirk Adamson, MBA. He was a great help and many of the early ideas for several chapters can be traced back to his work and efforts.

I would also like to thank all of my family, friends, and clients for their continued support throughout the years. Without you this book would not have been possible.

Finally, while there are scores of others that have had their hand in the process, without Henry, "The Hammer," and "Pooker" I am not sure if this would have ever been completed. You know who you are… Thanks!

Table of Contents

PREFACE

The reason I have dedicated so much time to writing this book is to provide you with the tools you need to make your financial dreams a reality. It is my hope is that you will take from these pages the important ideas that have helped so many others reach their personal financial goals. They have done this by simply utilizing the core investment practices explained in each chapter and now proudly consider themselves "Disciplined Investors."

As you begin to read this book you may find it beneficial to browse different sections rather than reading it straight through. It is by no means essential to read the material in the exact order in which the chapters are laid out. Rather, you can scan over most of the book in order to get a good understanding of how the information is presented. In fact, to save time during your initial scan, mark the pages you are most interested in—and then go back and <u>read them thoroughly</u>. After, focus on the chapter(s) that you found to be the most relevant to your particular situation, concentrating on the specific topics you want to master.

Along with a small amount of dedication and a large amount of desire, you are about to embark on the ultimate journey toward financial success.

Read on, Read on…

FOREWORD

Investors over the last two and a half decades have benefited from the greatest boom in history. Despite two strong crashes in 1987 and 2000 - 2002, stock returns have been higher than any time in U.S. history. The recent bubble in housing saw the greatest appreciation in history from 2000 - 2005. Outside of a few years in the early 1990s, most investors have never seen house prices go down for an extended period of time. But this bubble boom is coming to an end.

The massive baby boom generation has been driving this unprecedented boom as they simply aged–earning and spending more money and buying more houses and cars and etc. In the next decade they will be slowing in their spending—just as occurred in Japan in the 1990s and early 2000s. When this occurred in Japan, the Nikkei declined 80% between 1990 and 2003. There will not be increasing numbers of buyers for the McMansions the baby boomers own. This housing slump is not almost over, it is just starting. Home prices in Japan declined 60% from 1991 to 2005 when their baby boom aged past their peak spending years. The next generation will be looking for apartments and low cost starter homes. The explosion in technology trends is now close to saturating consumer households with wireless, Internet and broadband penetration at 80% of households in 2007 and approaching saturation at 90% by late 2008. The last time we saw such a powerful cluster of technologies saturate our economy was in 1928 -1929—just before the Great Depression.

The incredible gains in most investment trends have bailed many investors out of investment strategies that lacked planning, discipline and risk management. Managing risk and getting more realistic about returns will be much more critical to success in the next decade that will see even more volatility and more downside than upside.

In this book, Andrew Horowitz gives investors the proven planning and risk management tools to succeed in an increasingly challenging environment ahead. This is the time to get serious about your finances and your life plan—before this bubble really starts to burst, most likely between late 2008 and late 2010.

Harry S. Dent, Jr.
Author of *The Roaring 2000s* and forthcoming, *Bubble Boom, Bubble Bust*

Chapter 1

Creating a Discipline

"Where do I begin?" For some, this can prove to be a challenging question. For others, it can be so difficult to answer that it actually creates a kind of mental paralysis. It frustrates and annoys them to a level where they never begin a task in the first place. This same query represents the most often pondered question of the true procrastinator. To them, not starting is better than starting and never finishing.

Even if you are the most polished of procrastinators, the pages ahead will help guide you to success. With this book, we will work together, step by step, to formulate a detailed personal investment discipline. Whether you are a novice or seasoned investor looking to hone the skills you have acquired over the past few decades, there is something here for you.

No matter what your level of experience is, structuring a program with deliberation and discipline can only help you to become more successful. As time goes on you will also find it critical that you continue learning as the markets change.

Let us take a look at some examples of why an investment discipline can be worthwhile:

Ted, a retiree, has built a sizeable portfolio that he has been managing on his own for years. Until now, he has been relying on basic information supplied by his broker and obtained from newspapers and magazines. He has had the tendency to try to reinvent the wheel with each investment decision. Recently he has begun to realize that the daily investment process is taking up more of his free time than he would like.

One issue Ted faces is that many of his stocks carry a low **cost basis,** 📖 and he does not want to accept the tax implications when they are sold. In addition, he has been traveling more lately—and, as such, has been leaving his portfolio without daily management, which is creating another concern.

> 📖 **COST BASIS**
> The amount invested in a given security or portfolio. The formula is rather straightforward: Multiply the total shares that you have purchased by the share price. Next, add in any commissions paid. Tracking this is important; it is the indicator for figuring out if you are making or losing money. When you eventually sell the security, you will need this information to compute your taxes. For mutual funds, you need to add in all of the dividends and gains that have been reinvested.

Ted is the classic, modern-day investor. The rewards that come with the daily grind of managing his portfolio are bittersweet. On one hand, he enjoys the challenge. On the other, it drives him crazy. As his portfolio has grown, he has become less comfortable with handling it, yet he does not want to give up control.

For Ted, the problem lies in the fact that he does not have a model that he can reproduce. By creating price targets (see Chapter 4) and using covered calls (see Chapter 5), he could save himself the aggravation of experiencing excessive losses caused by holding on to investments for too long. He would finally be able to go on vacation without worrying that, in his absence, his portfolio might crash and burn.

By creating an appropriate asset allocation plan (see Chapter 9), he would have the ability to manage his assets logically without the emotional second-guessing most people encounter.

Here is another example:

Brandon and Emily are young, first-time investors that have no idea where to begin. They have met with several financial experts, yet they are not comfortable with any of them. They both feel that with some measure of effort, they are capable of building an investment plan for the long term. However, they lack the tools and knowledge to make decisions on individual mutual funds and stocks.

For these types of investors, a lesson in stock selection (see Chapters 3 and 4) along with an introduction to solid investment tools (see Chapters 2 and 8) will help them discover which stocks are appropriate to invest in. They should also plan to monitor their portfolio on an ongoing basis in order to compare relative performance. More likely than not, mutual funds will prove to be an appropriate choice, as they take some of the management responsibilities off of the investors' shoulders (see Chapter 6).

As we see from the examples above about people, just like you and me, **wealth**📖 is important. However, each of us sees it differently as it has a tendency to appear in many shapes and sizes. Make no mistake—it is not solely related to money and finances. Those who believe it *is* usually end up losing in the investment game due to greed.

📖 WEALTH
Pronunciation: 'welth' also 'weltth'
Function: noun
Etymology: Middle English welthe, from wele weal
Date: 13th century
1: obsolete : WEAL, WELFARE
2: abundance of valuable material possessions or resources
3: abundant supply : PROFUSION
4a: all property that has a money value or an exchangeable value
b: all material objects that have economic utility; especially: the stock of useful goods having economic value in existence at any one time <national wealth>

(Source: Merriam Webster Dictionary)

Through the many studies conducted on the subject of investing, it is now known that the mentality and perception of money and the definition of wealth have dramatically changed over the past 25 years. According to a 1980s survey conducted by The American Council on Education, 75 percent of the 200,000 incoming college freshmen polled felt that being well off financially was either "an essential" or "a very important end" to achieve. In addition, 71 percent of the students said that the primary reason they were going into college was to attain high-paying jobs upon graduation.

Unfortunately, however, only 29 percent of those aspiring young people believed that it was necessary to develop a meaningful philosophy on life. That is, at best, a very troubling statistic.

Today's mentality has many people believing that money is easily acquired. If they lose some now, they can always recoup it later. Warren Buffett, one of the world's most respected investors, has simple yet sage-like advice on this subject. He says, "The first rule is not to lose money. The second rule is not to forget the first rule."

With that in mind, this book does not present the stock market as a fast track toward riches. Yet for many the various markets remains the most well-known and often-utilized area in which to accumulate wealth. While it is true that time has effectively and thoroughly tested the validity of that statement, do not make the mistake of thinking that what was will always be.

Have you taken notice that our world has very recently changed? Unless you have been hiding in a cold, dark cave, you realize that information is available to everyone, everywhere, at any time. Just think back to a few years ago, when a fax machine was the quickest way to exchange documents on an "I need it now" basis.

Fax machines are now considered old technology designed to provide paper-based documents for those who still do not have the ability or desire to utilize digitized files. The recent shift from "overnight" to "immediate" has taken place in a period of less than five years—astounding even the most technologically astute visionaries.

The ultimate price for this gift has *not* been the desired actualization of increased quality of life. Rather, it has transformed us into a species that has adopted an always-on mentality, which has us moving at record speeds 24 hours a day, 7 days a week, 52 weeks a year. The Internet is always open with information flowing freely.

At almost any given time of the day, some market around the world is open for investing. To top it off, information is being thrown at us from all sides, forcing us to believe that access now equals knowledge. Do you remember when you had to wait until the following day to find out at what price your stock closed? In those days, newspapers were the most common providers of post-market information.

Today it is a much different story. Most of us have our computers turned on and tuned in during market hours, enabling us to watch each and every tick of our investments.

The Internet phenomenon that began in 1995 caused a growing number of investors to believe that they could beat the odds and take the daily management of their portfolios into their own hands. Massive stock market gains forced a change to the risk assumptions that many investors had held on to for decades.

Then, almost overnight, it was as if a large number of the level-headed individuals among us were replaced with aliens from a world where money matters were a game. One of the rules must have required open discussions about investment triumphs (and the rarer story of a loss) at every opportunity. Dinner parties, weddings, breakfasts, and even shuffleboard games served as acceptable gathering places for mini-seminars.

Prosperity permeated the air and was coupled with an insatiable desire for wealth accumulation, which served as the primary catalyst for change.

People were talking about the greatest return they made that week while hiding from the obvious concern that they could actually lose money someday. Stories of the "old stock market" were banned from discussions as the "new era" of investing was clearly here to stay. Investigations and reports concerning excessively high price-to-earnings ratios that exceeded historic levels were often suppressed.

Resembling fully indoctrinated cult followers, no one seemed to want to ask questions—especially ones like, "Why is it so easy to make money?" or "When will it end?" Instead, innate greed brainwashed the masses, transforming investors into gamblers.

Anyone who threw caution to the wind eventually realized that there was a reason why many of the experts declared the markets overvalued and thus recommended looking toward other investment and diversification techniques. If you were one of the late players in the game, you know the fall from grace that started in March of 2000 was a severe one. Across the board, stocks lost a good part of the gains they made during the prior five years, and some mutual funds were cut down by 30 percent or more.

Not everyone got caught up in the frenzy, though. There were still a few on the sidelines, ever fearful of a repeat of the 1930s—but only a few. It *was* quite an extreme situation and it *was* very difficult to resist the temptation to get in on the action. After all, everyone was doing it.

Perhaps the very best way to explain why this bizarre situation occurred is with a somewhat real-life illustration. By considering the experiences of the following couple, we can identify the many influences that caused investors to fall prey to the frenzy. You also have the benefit of looking at the situation in hindsight—always a good perspective for analysis. From this vantage point, you can begin the process of appropriately building *your* disciplines.

Bob and Julie were making a good living, each working in their respective jobs for the previous decade or so. Both had 401(k) plans and had been employing the advice of a local financial planner, who gave them guidance on selecting mutual funds to help them plan for retirement as well as for college savings for their children.

One day, Bob was on the golf course with his buddies when he overheard a discussion about the latest **IPO**📖 that two of his friends had invested in. They had both turned $2,500 into $10,000 within a week. One friend even commented that IPOs were "like taking candy from a baby."

📖 **IPO (INITIAL PUBLIC OFFERING)**
The first stock sold by a company when it becomes a publicly traded entity. IPOs receive much more attention than they deserve, in part because the hottest IPOs can make their purchasers a quick profit by soaring soon after trading begins. This was especially true during the heat of the 1998-1999 bull market, when the acronym "IPO" seemed to stand for "Instant Profit Opportunity." For the most part, though, early gains usually disappear rather quickly. IPOs are risky investments, as they are usually represented by newer companies without proven track records.

Bob was intrigued. He asked his friend if he could speak to his broker and get in on the action. After all, he had extra monies "lying around." Bob's friend graciously introduced him to his broker, and, after purchasing a couple of profitable IPOs, Bob realized how easy it was to make money in the stock market in those days.

Then, after a few more "instant money" IPOs and fast-profit picks, Bob decided to give it a try on his own. He was anxious to build his portfolio so that both he and Julie could retire early. Julie was a little more skeptical, but she went along with Bob's idea since it truly was amazing how easy the transactions seemed to be.

Bob and Julie were both feeling great. The euphoria of controlling their own destiny was fantastic. Setting up an account with an online discount broker was easy for them since they were both comfortable and experienced with the Internet. Both of them had regularly used the Internet for shopping online. Trading seemed no different.

Within a day, Bob had started trading after work, gathering ideas from online bulletin boards and chat rooms. He also listened closely to the lunchtime discussions between his coworkers. In the beginning, it seemed that those people really knew what they were doing. Virtually everything they invested in made big money.

After about two months, both Bob and Julie remarked that their brokerage statements were looking very different than they used to. The percentages of increase were climbing at a record rate. One night, they talked it over and decided that since their financial advisor had "only" been providing them annual returns approaching 12 percent during the past 10 years, he would have to be replaced by the new "online money tree."

At the same time, they decided without hesitation to invest all of their excess income and all of the money they had in savings accounts into the stocks that had showed such incredible momentum during the previous few months.

Increasingly, much of Bob's time during the day was spent watching the computer screen rather than keeping his focus on his job and the obligation he had to his employer. Julie even acquired the online passcodes she needed to sneak a peak at the portfolio each day and see how it was doing.

After a while, the couple decided to buy what was "hot" without looking any further into the fundamentals of a company's products or management. They felt that "old-fashioned" research was no longer required. It took up a great deal of time and it did not seem to help anyway.

Bob and Julie were flying high. These new-world investments surely beat their day jobs. Why bother working so hard, in an effort to retire in a few years, when assets could be built up so quickly and easily within a portfolio?

Each time the market dipped, they decided to devote additional monies, even arranging for a second mortgage on their house in order to invest more into the markets. At that point, Bob and Julie learned about **margin borrowing**📖 as a tool to leverage their buying power—thereby allowing the couple to make even more fast money.

Ignoring all advice from their now almost-forgotten financial advisor and any negative possibilities being painted against the backdrop of prosperity, they both found new religion in the process. They proudly and openly proclaimed that this would be the norm.

📖   MARGIN BORROWING
Brokerage companies are allowed to lend money to investors at reasonable rates. These loans are collateralized against the stocks in the borrower's account. When an investor uses margin to buy securities, they are leveraging the purchase, which can be a great benefit if the investments move up. If, on the other hand, the investments lose money, the downside effect is compounded. Add to that the fact that either way there is a cost to borrow funds. That cost needs to be included in the calculation to determine your gain or loss.

The improper use of margin has been credited to the stock market crash of 1929. Since then, strict regulations have been implemented to ensure that investors use margin with more care.

Most recall what happened next, but for for those that do not, here are the gory details:

It was March 2000 when the first major "dip" began to take shape. That time, though, things were going to be different. At first, Bob and Julie were comfortable with the notion that this dip, like the others, was going to be temporary. They thought it would quickly bounce back and were confident it was nothing to worry about. A month went by. Things were still not looking so good.

Getting close to a **margin call**, Bob and Julie agreed to stop trading for a while, as they were starting to have some doubt about their holdings. After a few months, they received their first margin call, requesting that monies be deposited to their accounts in order to cover the loans that they had used to buy stocks. Now down by over 30 percent, the only thing for them to do was to hold...right?

📖 MARGIN CALL

A requirement for additional capital in order to strengthen the equity in an investor's margin account. Let us suppose that you purchased 500 shares of ABC stock, which cost you $2,000. Before the buy, your account was worth $1,000; therefore you borrowed $1,000 from the brokerage company on margin in order to pay for the transaction. Now, if the stock were to fall by 10%, there would be a shortfall in the account minimum margin requirement, and you would be forced to either sell a part of the position or deposit funds to bring the amount back to the required level. Since the lending rate is generally a maximum of 50%, once the value of ABC stock goes down there will be a "Call" for the money due.

While there *were* a few **bear market bounces**, by the time the year closed out Bob and Julie's investment portfolio had fallen by more than 55 percent. They had no idea of what to do next. Their friends no longer talked about investments while playing golf. Conversations were spotted with the salient confessions of losses suffered.

Portfolios heavy with relatively worthless holdings had become the common achievement of this wild ride. The tide had turned, and all those who did not heed the warnings of the past had thrown up their hands in shamed surrender.

📖 BEAR MARKET BOUNCE

A temporary recovery by a market after a prolonged decline or "bear market." In most cases, the recovery is only temporary. Also known as a Dead Cat Bounce—a term derived from the rather ugly old saying that "even a dead cat will bounce if it is dropped from high enough."

In the end, a growing number of investors who were financially ruined went back to tried-and-true methods that were developed over decades. These included risk management, asset allocation, and research. In other words, they began to look for <u>disciplines</u>.

Hopefully we have all learned a valuable lesson from this catastrophe. It is a message that is asking us to open our eyes, ears, and minds to the possibilities of a dynamically changing investment climate.

Let us make something clear from the start: a discipline is a process that is ever evolving; one that is designed to help enhance market returns and limit risk. Disciplines can be used on their own as devices to filter stocks or in conjunction with each other, to find investments that work in concert within a portfolio.

A discipline should not be used as an excuse to blindly follow strategies that may have worked over the previous 12 months. It is not a process that is sold to you by a stockbroker intending to help keep you out of the investment process altogether.

Investment disciplines originate from a myriad of sources that utilize varied techniques to find investments for different purposes. While that may seem like a very broad comment, the idea will become clearer to you as you read on. Together, we are going to define what strategies work best for your particular investment style. These will help to further identify your risk characteristics and eventually lead toward specific investments in stocks, bonds, mutual funds, and other areas that will enable you to diversify a portfolio for the long haul.

Some call a diversified portfolio of this type an "All-Weather Portfolio"; others think of it as a "Balanced Investment Style." Whatever the catch-phrase, the combined results will allow for less worrying on your part and a greater understanding of why your portfolio is performing the way it is.

Perhaps you can personally identify with Bob and Julie. Maybe you have been so astute as to convert your portfolio entirely to cash right before the market corrected. Or perhaps you are somewhere in the middle, looking for an answer to the question of how to prosper in the long run.

Either way, it is time to make a commitment to open up your senses to all possibilities and all options. Rid yourself of any preconceived notions that you have about what a broker does, how the markets operate, and what your role is in the process. Pack them up and put them aside just for a moment, so that you may discover another truth—one in which you are no longer shackled to a computer screen or a financial news program; one that will ultimately allow you to create a system that efficiently promotes wealth accumulation. Once you find that truth it should become the essence of the disciplines you will use as a guide on your quest towards prosperity.

The poignant lesson that we should have learned from Bob and Julie is best highlighted by a famous story. Remember the

Aesop fable about the goose and the golden egg? It is the story of a poor farmer who one day visited the nest of his prized goose, finding at her side a glittering, yellow egg. Convinced that it must have been a trick, he was about to throw it away before he quickly changed his mind…but he didn't.

He decided to take the egg home for analysis. To his delight, he discovered that the egg was pure gold. The farmer became fabulously rich by gathering one golden egg every day from the nest of his special goose. As he grew richer, he became greedier and more impatient. Hoping to secure all the gold at once, he killed the goose and opened her, only to find nothing inside.

What can be learned from this story is that growth is a daily grind composed of successes, failures, lost opportunities, progress, and change. Thinking that wealth can be attained in one fell swoop is dangerous and often results in losing a fortune.

The next task is to find out about your overall investment preferences. A **risk tolerance** assessment is a good place to start.

📖   RISK TOLERANCE

Best defined as the amount of psychological pain you are willing to endure from your investments.

For example, if your risk preference is high, you might feel fairly comfortable investing in options contracts or other investments that are very volatile. The preference for lower risk would lead you toward more conservative investments that do not tend to have large fluctuations in value. Some also call this your "sleep factor."

The best way to go about this is to look at yourself from the outside in. Take a moment to answer the following questions:

1) What is my age and family status (at what point will I need this money)?
2) Is the money subject to penalties upon withdrawal? (IRAs, pensions, annuities, etc.)
3) What are my tax considerations regarding this portfolio?
4) What is the likelihood that I can replace this money if I lose some or all of it?
5) What is my experience with investing on my own?
6) How much time am I willing to put into this process on an ongoing basis?
7) Do I have access to the tools that I need in order to manage and monitor my investments?
8) Who else should be involved in the decision-making process?

When you have these questions answered, utilize them to develop a paragraph or two about your investment goals. This self-assessment statement will help you stay focused and committed to your investment goals. Yes, this means that you should take out a pen and paper and actually write them down. I learned very early on in my career that goals and other important ideas are not worth the breath they ride on if they are not committed to paper. Hence, the creation of this book.

A sample self-assessment statement might look like this:

I am 42, and my wife is 40. We have 2 children (ages 11 and 8). For the most part, the funds we have in savings are going to be used for retirement. Some of the funds will also be needed to cover college costs. This money is not in an

*IRA or pension and will not have a penalty for withdrawal.
That means that the income and gains are taxable. Other
monies are in my company's pension plan.*

*Since my spouse and I are both working, we could replace
some of the monies that may be lost in investments—but
only up to a certain point. Our experience with investing is
limited to a few long-term mutual funds and our company
pensions. As we are both busy people, we can only put in a
few hours per week at the most for investment purposes.
We are planning to make the decisions jointly and have the
tools through our broker to track the investments.*

The above represents a good starting point for you to begin
crafting your statement in the space provided on Page 27.
After writing your statement you should be well on your way
to better understand just what type of investor you are. For
further clarification, see Figure 1 as it provides a good
sampling of risk styles.

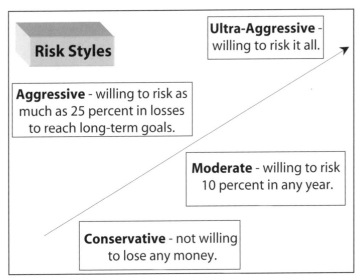

Figure 1

If you are married or in another otherwise committed relationship, a great way to further refine your style is to read the statement aloud to your significant other. He or she may have additional or conflicting thoughts about how much risk they are willing to take. You may find out more than you bargained for when you ask about their thoughts on the subject. In fact, more often than not, couples find out very late in their relationships how they really feel about money and finance.

Once you know your particular investment style, it is time to explore the core ingredients of a discipline. For the moment, we will stay with the example of the couple in the sample self-assessment statement. They have a moderate risk tolerance level.

Realize that even the most tightly wound discipline is not without its pitfalls. Regardless of the area that you choose to focus your investment agenda upon, your portfolio will face risks.

First, risks exist well beyond the loss of principal due to market fluctuations. However, loss of principal is where most investors stop when they think of risk. Over time, **inflation**📖 plays a key part in diminishing the spending power of your money. Just think about an investment such as a CD that consistently earns 3.5 to 4 percent annually. Over time, the investment will grow substantially. In fact, at a 3.5 percent annual rate of return, money doubles in approximately 20.5 years. This also means that when using that same rate for inflation, money *loses* 50 percent of its value every 20.5 years.

📖   INFLATION RISK

The risk that our money will not be worth as much in the future. It is expected that the cost of the things we need to buy (such as housing, clothing, and medical care) will all increase.

Low-yield investments (such as guaranteed investments and bank accounts) usually do not keep pace with inflation.

Next is **currency risk,** 📖 though it is usually not a concern for those investing exclusively in dollar-denominated investments. Years ago it was not as easy to buy non-dollar-denominated investments. These days, they can easily be obtained through investments in mutual funds. This potentially adds an additional level of risk for those mutual funds that have exposure to the foreign markets.

📖 CURRENCY RISK

This term refers to the risk imposed on an investment by fluctuating worldwide currency exchange rates. When you invest in the mutual funds or stocks of companies that are overseas, there is an inherent risk associated with owning the investment in a foreign currency. Once the investment is sold and the money is eventually converted back to U.S. dollars, there may be an additional loss or gain depending on the current exchange rate. Mutual funds face this risk when investing as well. In order to reduce some of the risk, they employ "hedging" to reduce the effects that the adverse exchange rate will have on the portfolio's performance.

Similarly, political instability risk has been a significant problem for many investors who have had money in regions such as Latin America and the Middle East. When governments are in conflict, it usually causes nervousness amongst investors, often to the detriment of financial markets.

This can also happen to investments in the U.S. stock markets. Consider, for example the hotly contested presidential race of November 2000 that caused chaos within the markets.

Without a clear winner, investors became worried over the outcome and looked at it as a sign of domestic weakness. The S&P 500 index lost 7.88 percent in that month alone.

Finally, since taxes are levied upon monies earned by investments, the net effect is the reduction in overall profits. Even if there is tax deferral through an annuity or a retirement plan, there will come a day when the government will collect its due share. Upwards of 30 to 40 percent of the total value of a portfolio may be confiscated by taxes over time. If nothing else, that should make you stand up and take notice, especially when considering the added effect of inflation and the significant impact it will have on the long-term value of any investment.

Portfolio Tax Comparison

	Tax *Efficient*		Tax *Inefficient*	
Start of Year Portfolio Value	$ 100,000.00		$ 100,000.00	
Income from Funds	$ 3,000.00	3.00%	$ 6,000.00	6.00%
Income from Stocks	$ 2,000.00	2.00%	$ 3,250.00	3.25%
Capital Gains from Funds	$ 1,250.00	1.25%	$ 4,000.00	4.00%
Additional *Unrealized* Capital Gains *·N/T*	$ 10,000.00	10.00%	$ 3,000.00	3.00%
Gross Gain	$ 16,250.00	16.25%	$ 16,250.00	16.25%
Tax on Gains	$ 1,650.00	*1.65%*	$ 3,390.00	*3.39%*
After-Tax (net) Portfolio Gain	$ 14,600.00	**14.60%**	$ 12,860.00	**12.86%**
Inflation-Adjusted Return	$ 14,162.00	14.16%	$ 12,474.20	12.47%

* Example shows fund and stock income taxed at 28%; fund gains taxed at 20% (average); N/T=Non-taxable; Inflation Assumption of 3% - Dividends may receive preferential treatment and tax rates will vary.

Further adding insult to injury is the fact that, when you die, there are potential estate taxes that can further reduce the wealth that you have worked so hard to amass. While there *was* a significant tax reform act passed in 2001, and more recently,

in 2006, the far-reaching implications of the changes will continue to tax your beneficiaries down the road.

Given all of these considerations, why in the world would
anyone open themselves up to so many negative possibilities?
Wouldn't it be better to leave the monies in a safe place at a
lower interest rate to avoid most of this hassle? The answer is
an unequivocal "No." This is because the opportunity to diversify a position of stocks, bonds, and mutual funds with
differing currency exposures, maturities, sectors, and industries
(along with investment styles and size diversification) can provide you with the opportunity to increase the probability of
positive returns while at the same time reducing the potential
risk.

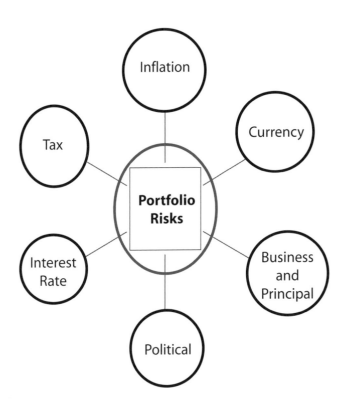

The good news is there are several ways in which you can reduce risk to a point that is manageable and acceptable. Chapter 9 covers the asset allocation process and points out how it can work in tandem with a disciplined investment strategy to create the potential for a highly stable and profitable portfolio. For now, it is safe to stick with the notion that risk is a topic that needs to be properly approached and defended against. Remember: there are many different types of risk that affect portfolios in just as many varying ways.

Now that you have a relatively good idea of what risk really is, let us go back to our example of Bob and Julie. When focusing closely on their risk assessment, we find that the money is in an account that is held outside the umbrella of a retirement plan. Therefore, the tax status of an account needs to be considered in order to protect the portfolio from erosion due to taxes.

Since they are relatively young, care needs to be taken in order to ensure that their investments keep pace with, and exceed, inflation. College costs are on the near horizon, so for that block of money safer, non-volatile investments should be utilized. It is probably accurate to say that they are moderate risk takers, as they are willing to lose some money in the pursuit of their goals.

This now leads directly to the point of actual investment types. Bob and Julie desire the greatest tax efficiency and lowest volatility. Therefore, individual equities will play an important role in this portfolio. In order to properly understand this, it is important to let go of any preprogrammed ideas you may have about individual stocks.

Over the years, mutual fund companies have attempted to create a mystique about the investment process. In particular, they have brilliantly convinced us that there are problems with investors using individual stocks within their portfolios. Large brokerage houses have heavily promoted the use of mutual funds for the average investor, as their number one priority has been asset gathering rather than investment management.

It has been startlingly easy to convince most consumers that mutual funds are better for them. Why wouldn't they be? There are "professionals" tending to the assets.

A number of years ago, John Bogle, founder of the Vanguard group of funds, wanted to find out if active management of a mutual fund provided returns greater than the index that they competed against. He discovered a significant under-performance by active managers as compared to their benchmark. He then set out to provide investors with a low-cost alternative to investing in the indices—the same ones that were beating the managers handily.

Vanguard's mantra of low expense ratios, low turnover, and a **passive management style**📖 turned the industry on its head. A few years later, Bogle's mutual fund company grew into one of the largest fund companies employed by individuals and institutional advisors. This was primarily due to a clear understanding that there should be no "hiding" of the fund's true investment policy and that, above all, it was essential to put the investor first.

📖 PASSIVE MANAGEMENT STYLE
A financial strategy in which a fund manager makes as few portfolio changes as possible in order to reduce transaction costs and minimize capital gains taxes. A very popular way to

achieve the same return as an index is to buy an index mutual fund. These types of funds utilize a passive management style and simply buy the same investments that are held within the index they are imitating. The managers of index funds do not have much work to do other than to ensure the fund maintains their absolute correlation with its benchmark index.

Clearly, mutual funds play an important role in a portfolio. They are most appropriate for the portfolio of investors with limited monies available to start a savings program. There is no better way to begin a **systematic investment plan**📖 than to stick to a monthly plan of investment through a fund. Even so, when it comes to proper diversification, it should be pointed out that there are many opportunities beyond a simple mutual fund. This will become much clearer when reading Chapter 6, where you will find more information about the tax inefficiency of most mutual funds and the inability of most fund managers to compete with a non-managed index.

📖   SYSTEMATIC INVESTMENT PLAN
A way in which an investor saves money for college, retirement, or other major life events by automatically investing in mutual funds on a monthly basis. Most plans start as low as $25 per month.

At this point, it is important to realize that one of the best uses of a mutual fund is for your international stock, domestic and international bonds as well as small cap stock exposures.

You may be thinking: I am scared of individual stocks, or, I have never purchased a stock in my life. I do not know the first thing about them. Not to worry. Armed with the information contained within the next few chapters, you will have all the tools needed to compete with the experts.

As a general rule, you should know that with every 10 percent of exposure to equities/stocks, your portfolio will also carry a volatility of 1 percent. For example, a portfolio comprised of 50 percent stocks and 50 percent bonds should have a volatility of 5 percent greater than a portfolio that carries nothing but bonds.

This is just one of many general rules that can be applied to a successful investment strategy. Until you identify your own needs, however, it will be impossible to effectively lay the foundation for your unique portfolio.

If we were to stop right here and lay out a plan to invest with the information we know up to this point, Bob and Julie's portfolio might look like this:

Individual Stocks	
Large-cap	20%
Mid-cap	10%
Mutual Funds	
Bonds/Fixed Income	30%
Small-cap	10%
International	20%
Cash/Other	10%

This allocation is overly simplistic and is for illustrative purposes only.

Building a Discipline

Every investor—with his or her many passions, carefully culti-vated biases, and unique inklings—is vastly different from all the others. The truly intriguing aspect of this statement is that, despite all of these separate conditions, there is a unified, underlying strategy to any successful portfolio. It is a concept that is based on discipline, analysis, shrewd and careful investment choices, a dash of independent ingenuity, and a reasonable tolerance for risk.

The key to understanding how to win in the markets does not come from a glitzy CD-ROM or an all-encompassing program with catchy phrases and "trade-secret" stratagems. While it is true that this journey is best traveled with the company of a qualified advisor, it can indeed be braved alone. The trick is to maintain a consistent investment discipline.

So how do you avoid procrastination, stagnation, or just plain poor decision making? The first step is to remove all emotion from the investment picture. For many of us, this is easier said than done. Fortunately, years of research and trial and error have lead to the development of exactly the kind of strategy it takes to invest without the bias of feelings or intuition.

The initial step is to apply a three-headed plan of careful analysis—the first of which you will find in the next chapter, Quantitative Analysis.

My Self-Assessment Statement

Chapter 2

Quantitative Analysis

Emotions play an important role in our everyday lives. People's instincts usually "alert" them to avoid certain foods, situations, and sometimes other people that they believe may be harmful. Surely you have had those "gut feelings" that seem as real as the air you breathe. There are even people who rely on their "intuition" to make many important decisions.

Whatever you want to call it—a hunch, an instinct, a premonition, or even a sixth sense—there is no room for this type of mentality in an investment discipline based on quantitative analysis.

Have you even been investing in a stock and said to yourself, "It just does not feel right," or "I really think that this is going to be a winner"? That enthusiasm or fear is an emotional response to information that we, as humans, are processing. The reaction is filtered through a host of preconceptions and learned behaviors that have built up throughout our lifetimes.

As people enter into new situations, their brains instantly call back historical memories, allowing them to access records that have been neatly stored in the infinitely complex corridors of the mind. Within a microsecond, a judgement is locked in about new circumstances that is based on these historical files and thus forms a prediction that is *believed* to be true. In the world of psychology, this is termed "classical conditioning."

Classical conditioning is a type of learning in which an animal's natural response to an object or sensory stimulus transfers to another stimulus. This is how a dog can learn to salivate at the sound of a tuning fork, an experiment first carried out in the early 1900s by Russian psychologist Ivan Pavlov.

The human brain has been compared to a machine that captures, processes, files, and then accesses information when needed, but not everyone believes that it is that simple. There is a group of scientists that believe people will look at their memories in a way that best suits their needs, drawing from their internal thoughts, desires, requirements, and past experiences. They also believe people use learned behaviors to help create assumptions and mold their memories to what they presume to be true.

Sometimes, without any malicious intent, people will even remember events differently from how they really happened. When two or more people are asked about an event that they witness simultaneously, vastly different memories of the situation are often reported.

Psychologists have studied and been fascinated with this phenomenon. In one study, "The Misinformation Effect Experiment," conducted by Elizabeth Loftus in 1978, subjects watched a slide show depicting a car accident. Randomly, they were shown either a "stop" sign or a "yield" sign in the slides. Immediately after, they were asked a question about the accident that implied the presence of the other sign that was not actually there. Influenced by this suggestion, many subjects recalled the incorrect traffic sign.

Another study conducted in July of 1995 by Henry L. Roediger III and Kathleen B. McDermott and reported in *The Journal of Experimental Psychology: Learning, Memory and Cognition* showed how people who listened to a list of sleep-related words (bed, yawn) or music-related words (jazz, instrument) were often convinced moments later that they had also heard the words "sleep" or "music"—words that fit the category but were not on the list.

This memory distortion effect was shown once again in another study where college students were asked to recall their high school report cards. Researchers checked those memories against the students' actual grades. While most of the grades were recalled correctly, many of the errors reported were exaggerations of the quality of the grades, especially when the actual ones were very low.

These examples are primary reasons why the quantitative ("quant") investment process was designed. For the most part, people will create preconceived notions about a stock based on its name, industry, sector, and even the location of the company's corporate offices. This can often bias the outcome of the recommendation if the analyst or the investor is not aware of their mental predisposition.

Quantitative analysis attempts to remove the emotional side of the process by means of filters, screens, and searches that are based on historical facts. Quants—those who ascribe to quantitative stock theory—believe that active management, technical analyses, fundamental analyses, or any combination of these three approaches are complete wastes of time. In fact, hardcore Quants would rather have a computer provide all of the stock picking recommendations, buying, selling, and reporting instead of an actual person. For them, human interaction adulterates the process and causes degradation of the byproduct of their efforts.

What is more, they believe that active "thinking" should be used during the *creation* of the technique, not after it is put into action. This is simply because the screen or filter needs to maintain its integrity by sticking to the original methodology. Only then can success be realized.

With that in mind, realize a compromise of methodologies is probably the better model for a *Disciplined Investor*. As you know by now, there are a host of tools that you need to possess in order to achieve success. Quant analysis is the filtering tool that will help you narrow down the list of potential stocks to include in your portfolio.

As there are literally tens of thousands of stocks available in the domestic stock markets, there needs to be a way to navigate through the chaos and find a few opportunities that can be further analyzed and reviewed. The truth is that no one person can efficiently research hundreds of stocks simultaneously. To do so would require a team of seasoned professionals to help gather, examine, and authenticate the data for further review.

For this reason, your practice of quantitative investing should be limited to the use of screening tools that will help to better refine the arduous task of searching through the available stock universe. These tools may also be used in the application of stock selection within a portfolio. This is often a hard task, as most investors despise taking losses and usually sell too early. This can help to push out losers without the emotional overlay.

Further, most investors have propensities toward one sector or another, as they often have a good deal of knowledge about their professional fields and the companies within them. This may helps provide an understanding of the sales cycles and trends for that stock group, but usually not for others.

So, if *you* feel that after reviewing all of the possible investment styles you have a better ability to research and make decisions on technology and growth-oriented stocks, then you may want to employ a quantitatively designed process in order to manage stock outside of these sectors.

Often, when a quantitative process is begun, the designer will seek out historical evidence on the performance of a basic, central element that is similar within a group of stocks. For instance, the Dogs of the Dow is a popular quantitative process that was introduced by Michael O'Higgins in 1991 in his book *Beating the Dow*. He discovered it as he was looking for a consistent and measurable system of stock selection that outperformed the Dow Jones Industrial Average (DJIA) annually. Similarly, an initial search criterion that you construct may be based on a simple filter.

Screens and criteria may be complex or simple—however, neither will end up being the ultimate cause of their success or failure. The Dogs of the Dow is a very simple process that calls for the buying of an equal dollar amount of the 10 stocks with the highest yields from the DJIA. They are to be held for a period of one year, at which time the screen is reevaluated. At that time, you find the 10 stocks with the highest yields again, sell any of the stocks that are no longer on the top 10 list, and replace them with the new "highest-yielders."

This method is dubbed the Dogs of the Dow because the high yielding stocks are the ones with prices that are low relative to the dividends paid, indicating stocks that are potentially out of favor.

James O'Shaughnessy provides one of the longest backtests in the book *What Works on Wall Street.* From December 1928 through December 2003, the Dogs returned 14.3 percent per year on average (12.2 percent when annualized), outperforming the S&P 500 which returned 11.7 percent on average (9.7 percent annualized).

For the 25-year period ending in 2005, this simple approach has compounded at an annual rate of over 18 percent, beating the DJIA and most professional money managers decisively. Interestingly, the string of annual wins was abruptly halted in the late 1990s as the relative performance leadership changed and returns on technology stocks trounced stocks in most other sectors.

Performance Comparison

| | 2002 | 2003 | 2004 | Ending December 2004 | | |
				1 Year	3 Year	10 Year
Dogs of the Dow	- 8.90%	28.70%	4.40%	4.40%	8.10%	12.90%
Small Dogs of the Dow	- 10.70%	23.50%	12.40%	12.40%	8.40%	12.10%
Dow Jones Industrial Average	- 15.00%	28.30%	5.30%	5.30%	6.20%	14.40%
S&P 500	- 22.10%	28.70%	10.90%	10.90%	5.80%	14.00%

(Source: Compiled from www.dj.com)

As an investor, there is an important issue to contend with when using a repetitive process that may trigger significant turnover within a portfolio. While deep-discount brokers are charging relatively low prices for trades, after a while the fees *do* add up. Also, tax implications need to be taken into consideration when buying and selling on a regular basis.

If you stick to a strict quantitative process and it triggers a sale, as a true Quant you will not override the recommendation simply because of tax implications. For some, this can represent a high price to pay for investing with this technique. This is especially true with some of the more complex strategies that can be developed. The more often there is the requirement for **rerunning a screen,** 📖 the greater the number of trades that will take place in your portfolio.

The Dogs of the Dow approach requires only an annual review and, as such, the costs associated with turnover and taxes are limited. Be careful, though—if you utilize a strategy and reset the portfolio prior to the expiration of 12 months, you may be required to pay a higher tax rate on the short-term, rather than the long-term, gains.

📖   RERUNNING A SCREEN
Some screens will require daily processing to choose portfolio positions. Fortunately, computers do most if not all of the heavy lifting.

One final story related to this type of investing before getting into the nuts and bolts and the actual technique:

Janus, the Roman god of doorways, gates, beginnings, and endings, reminds us of the importance of seeing the past as well as the future. The many statues and pictures of Janus portray him as having eyes, a nose, and a mouth on both the front and back of his head to show that doorways simultaneously include both entrances and exits. As he stands in the doorway—the present—he can look forward and backward at the same time. The month of January is named after this god, as it indicates the end of the old year and the beginning of the new one.

Taking Janus's advice, you can learn from where you have been while keeping your eyes focused on where you are going.

Understanding market history is an essential part of making sound investment decisions. The quantitative investment process relies solely upon history to validate its worth.

With this bit of information comes many pitfalls that you need to be able to recognize. First and foremost, quality of data is probably the most important component for ensuring worthwhile results. Great care needs to be taken when finding data sources that will allow us to gain a level of accuracy and comfort. This point will be addressed frequently because for this process to work, data integrity is an absolute necessity.

Second, a clear head that is unbiased in implementing the process will give you the best opportunity for success. Earlier you read the discussion about the strict Quants and their desire to have computers run the entire system. As much as possible, you need to allow technology to take over while you act as the controller of the inputs. When creating a new screen or recreating an existing one, make sure that you are wide awake, and take your time.

Beyond the essential need for data integrity, the time horizon for the testing of results should be as long as possible. The basic premise of this discipline is to find a recurring theme that identifies stocks that will outperform.

After the idea for a screen is generated, back-testing is important. That way you will be able to see how the inputs that you have chosen have performed over the years. The longer the time, the better the chances are that a pattern can be discerned through the noise. There have been studies that have gone back as far as 40 years just to prove that the design works.

To use four decades of information requires a great deal of data as well as an enormous amount of time and manpower. Years ago, the lack of available computer power was the biggest obstacle when performing a back-test. Today, this is no longer a problem.

For professionals, historical information is readily available, yet still expensive. Probably the best source for this information is the Standard & Poor's Compustat database. Unfortunately this service can cost a subscriber several thousands of dollars per year—surely not the most feasible option for an individual investor.

Finally, there is an inherent need for most people to find simple solutions. Everyone wants to win, and enthusiasm often gets in the way of our better judgment. Sometimes people look for rationales to justify data instead of looking toward the data to provide its own answers. This is what is known as data-mining. What ends up happening is novice investors believe they have the winning solution that will become the next great investment idea. Do not let this happen to you. Be skeptical. Assume that each new idea is a bad one until it is proven otherwise.

Over the course of the next few pages you will be presented with screens that have been thoroughly compiled and back-tested over a number of years. Each screen will include a step-by-step instruction set for its creation within *Microsoft's MSN Money* website (http://www.moneycentral.com). This is the best alternative to many of the high-cost professional data products.

You will first need to activate an account through Microsoft's online *Passport* or *Hotmail* system. Once you navigate to the *MSN Money* website, there will be an area to log in and create a new account. All of this is free, although you may receive periodic e-mails from Microsoft and their advertising affiliates.

Once you are set up, you can log in to the investor site (http://moneycentral.msn.com/investor). You will find that Microsoft's data sources and the overall ease of use is well suited for the purpose of stock screening.

Realize that there is no guarantee that each piece of data from this or any other source will be 100 percent accurate. That is the general rule when it comes to stock analysis and investigation, particularly when looking at historical information. You may be asking yourself, "Why is that?" It is purely because information is input by people, and sometimes people make mistakes. Also, with the ever-growing number of earnings restatements, dividend corrections, stock splits, mergers, acquisitions, and secondary offerings, information needs to be adjusted constantly—and it is not always done correctly.

While this *is* a scary thought, remember that these problems are present in *all* databases and therefore, you are still on a level playing field with even the most seasoned professionals.

There are a few items that you will need to become comfortable with as you start to use this excellent screening tool. It is important that you become familiar with the basic functions and features available to you, as they are extremely powerful.

For our purposes, it is assumed that you have a basic knowledge of the *MSN Money* website. If you don't, don't worry—what follows is a guide that will provide for most of the processes that you will need to master. As a warm-up, here is a quick lesson to help you get better acquainted with the screening system: *(Note: This requires installation of the MSN Money Investment Toolbox for Microsoft Internet Explorer)*

Download and install from either:
1) http://www.thedisciplinedinvestor.com or;
2) http://moneycentral.msn.com/investor/controls/FinderPro.asp)

    1) Go to http://www.moneycentral.com
    2) On the top navigation bar, click INVESTING
    3) Next, below, click STOCKS in the sub-menu
    4) On the left bar, click STOCK SCREENER and then click CUSTOM SEARCH
    5) Click below Field Name
    6) Select COMPANY BASICS and then DOW JONES MEMBERSHIP
    7) Click under OPERATOR, and then click an option
    8) Click " = "
    9) Click under VALUE, and then click an option

10) Use DJ INDUSTRIALS
11) Look for the box that says, "Return Top Matches"
12) Type in "30"
13) After you finish adding criteria, click RUN SEARCH

What you now have is a current list of the 30 stocks that make up the DJIA. As you see them, they are ranked in alphabetical order by the name of the company.

Tips

• If you click ASK ME in the Value field, you will be prompted to pick a value each time you run the search.

• If you click DISPLAY ONLY in the Operator field, the criterion will appear in the results, but it will not affect the search results.

• To remove a search criterion, right-click the gray box at the far left of the row, and then click DELETE ROW.

• To quickly reorder your results, click the column heading you want to sort by. Click the heading again to reverse the sort order.

• To adjust a column's width, click, hold down and drag the dividers between the column headings.

• To adjust the height of the panes, click and drag the split bar.

• To change the position of the columns, click a column heading and while holding it down drag it to a new location.

Remember, there are three basic components to be input for each screen: Field Name, Operator, and Value. These are the components that build the query that provides the results.

The only other area that you will need to enter anything into is under "Return Top Matches." This is a number (up to 100) that limits the query to the quantity of matching stocks you wish to see, based upon the criteria provided.

One more note: the addition of field names acts as an AND statement when searching through the available information. Translated, this means that *all* criteria must match in order to show up in the final result. This is different than an OR statement, which will bring out information from *either* Field Name input.

Above the Search1 title is the VIEW menu item. Click VIEW and a dropdown menu appears:

Within this submenu, you will find the option to choose "Column Set Displayed." Scroll down to "Company Basics" and select that as the layout.

You will now notice that the results pane has changed to include the most pertinent information regarding the companies in the search. Try a few more displays to get accustomed to the ones that are prepackaged with the system.

There is also a handy option that allows for the creation of an unlimited number of custom views. For the time being, stick with the predefined ones. In addition to this, there are predefined searches available to help get you thinking about some of your own ideas. Clicking on the "File" menu and choosing "Open" will display these.

This will then bring you to a screen that allows you to either open the screens that you have previously saved or open pre-designed stock and fund screens. To see what one actually looks like, select the "Dogs of the Dow" and then click "Open and Run." The result is the 10 highest dividend-paying stocks of the DJIA as compared to their prices.

Screens

Dogs of the Dow

The basic premise was discussed previously, so only the criteria and a few comments are provided here. Use the following table as a guide to inputting your screen. Match the fields, operators, and values to come up with the current list of "Dogs."

Dogs of the Dow

This is a great screen to uncover stocks that are super value-oriented. Because the current dividend yield is requested to be as high as possible, the price is obviously comparably low to what it may have been just a short time ago.

Field Name	Operator	Value
Dow Jones Membership	=	DJ Industrials
Current Dividend Yield	High as Possible	

The problem today is that there are now many stocks within the DJIA that provide little or no dividend. This means that they are repeatedly excluded as possible candidates in this screen.

Case in point: Microsoft and Intel were added to the DJIA in 2000 because it was believed that a change in the index composition was important to keep updated with the then-current investment climate. However, neither of these stocks had ever paid a dividend that was worth talking about. In fact, when it was initially included in the DJIA, Microsoft had never paid a dividend, as management believed that investing back into the company was a better way to go. At that time, Intel's dividend yield was a paltry 0.30 percent.

Even if these two stocks are the worst performers in any given year, they will most assuredly be excluded from the final list of "Dogs." There is virtually no chance that they will ever be included in this list.

As a matter of fact, 10 out of the 30 stocks that make up the index maintain a dividend yield of less than 1 percent. Consequently, screening from this universe will essentially result in 10 Dogs out of 20, rather than 10 out of 30.

Price-to-Sales for Large-Cap Stocks

In his acclaimed book *What Works on Wall Street,* Jim O'Shaughnessy states, "The price-to-sales ratio is the king of all the value factors." He goes on to explain that this individual value ratio has been the best performer throughout history. In fact, his research shows that using this one criterion helped investors beat the markets more than with any other value ratio, and did so more consistently.

The Large-Cap Price-to-Sales screen will provide you with an excellent list of value stocks that can be combined with other ideas. For the most part, the outcome of the query will reveal those companies that have a high level of sales but have not seen their stock price appreciate commensurately.

The implication is that stocks here have lower downside potential, as they have a respectable stream of revenue that may eventually be rewarded. This is a far cry from those go-go growth stocks with high prices and low sales. While the upside for those is great, the downside is usually even greater.

Large-Cap Price-to-Sales

Field Name	Operator	Value
S&P Index Membership	=	S&P 500
Market Capitalization	High as Possible	
Price-to-Sales Ratio	Low as Possible	

While simple, the results may provide you with an interesting list of candidates to think about researching further. Most of the results will represent value-oriented stocks by the very nature of the criteria used. Some, on the other hand, may actually be "diamonds in the rough."

S&P Index Slugs (SAPI Slugs)
According to MSN Money, this simple but effective value search presents a pure yield play. It is similar but potentially superior to the better-known "Dogs of the Dow" search we

just received because it draws from a wider pool of large-cap stocks and includes a secondary financial-strength overlay.

The search was also developed and tested by money manager and author Jim O'Shaughnessy. The strategy calls for buying the top 20 stocks from the result set of this search, ranked by dividend yield. These should be held for 1 year and then rescreened and rebalanced. It can be combined with O'Shaughnessy's Momentum Growth search to create a balanced 30-stock, 1-year portfolio. This search criteria and others are available in the *stock screener* section of the *MSN Money* website and can also be downloaded from *The Disciplined Investor* website (www.thedisciplinedinvestor.com).

The theory of using more than one screen is to allow for greater diversification within the portfolio. This way, if one particular screening method is sorely out of favor, the other may help to avoid massive losses.

In his research, O'Shaughnessy built portfolios for one year each. Translated, this means that once you buy the resulting stocks and effectively hold them for 52 weeks, you can rerun the screen to find the stocks to include in the next cycle.

For most individual investors, this is a tedious task and can result in excessive trading fees. Also, as has been discussed, the tax implications alone could be extremely detrimental to a portfolio's performance. This is precisely why these methods are often used within tax-deferred accounts along with additional fundamental overlays. Suffice it to say that these screens should be used as initial idea generators, not as absolute methodologies.

SAPI Slugs

Field Name	Operator	Value
S&P Index Membership	=	S&P Industrials
Current Dividend Yield	High as Possible	1,000,000
Market Capitalization	>=	
Current Ratio	>=	Industry Average Current Ratio
Debt/Equity Ratio	<=	Industry Average Debt/Equity Ratio
Industry Name	Display Only	

The *MSN Money* stock-screening tool makes available some great ways to unearth buried opportunities. One that has been found to be very profitable in an upward momentum bull market is The Earnings Momentum and Analyst Upgrades screen, which searches out the information reported by seasoned analysts.

Earnings Momentum and Analyst Upgrades
This particular screen is meant to be used as a brainstorming tool for those stocks that may be possible short- to mid-term momentum plays. The very thought that analysts are raising their assumptions can cause the sentiment surrounding a stock to quickly change. As has been seen from the bull markets that occurred during the latter part of the 1990s, earning surprises both to the upsides and downsides have a habit of creating either prosperity or poverty.

When an analyst that closely studies a certain company or sector changes his or her rating or earnings estimate for that company or sector, it is a pretty good sign that there is something more going on than meets the eye. Companies such as Zacks Investment Research are in the business of following these analysts and tracking the changes that they make to their ratings and earnings estimates.

This search focuses on the companies with the highest earnings-per-share growth projected for the next year and for which the analysts have increased their estimates. It also adds additional parameters and overlays to find the stocks with the greatest recent price changes and upward-moving technical trends.

Momentum and Earnings Up

Field Name	Operator	Value
Earnings Estimate Increased	Since	<In the Last Month>
EPS Growth Next Year	High as Possible	
Previous Day's Closing Price	>=	50-Day Moving Average
% Price Change Last 6 Months	Display Only	

You will undoubtedly find many stocks that you have probably never heard of within these results. *Caveat emptor!* Try not to let yourself get sucked into the temptation of following historic returns. Be sure to keep a cool head and think about the company and its longer-term prospects.

GARP

Contrarian plays have long been attractive strategies for those investors who do not have the stomachs for high-ratio stocks. By their very nature, these types of strategies expose stocks that have fallen from grace within the eyes of the markets. They also find ones that have never caught fire while growing at rates appropriate to their underlying fundamentals.

Somewhere in between the world of growth and value investing is the GARP (growth at a reasonable price) patron. This theory, popularized by Acorn Fund manager Ralph Wanger (also the author of *A Zebra in Lion Country*), focuses on finding opportunities with a modest risk within the realm of smaller capitalization stocks. To control risk, Wanger advocates companies with proven management structures. He also looks for stocks with sound balance sheets and strong standings in their industries, while simultaneously avoiding those that are already overpriced.

Growth at a Reasonable Price (GARP)

Fieldname	Operator	Value
Market Capitalization	<=	1,000,000,000
Income Per Employee	>=	Industry Average Income Per Employee
Inventory Turnover	>=	Industry Average Inventory Turnover
Debt/Equity Ratio	<=	0.5
5-Year Revenue Growth	>=	20
EPS Growth Next 5 Years	High As Possible	
P/E Ratio Current	<=	EPS Growth Next 5 Years
PEG Ratio Below 1	True Now	

The information returned from this hybrid technique, which employs multiple levels of filters, will help find additional opportunities for investment. For the most part, looking at both the income per employee and the inventory turnover helps to seek out those companies that have an edge over their industry constituents.

Each of the resulting stocks from this screen likely reflects the company's ability to understand the distribution and manufacturing process of the goods they are selling.

When a company consistently shows the ability to be a leader within these two important areas, there may be something further to review.

Debt to equity is very important to keep at a minimum, especially in smaller companies. The impact of large debt loads are most pronounced with small-cap firms. As this screen hunts for companies with market capitalization of under $1 billion, this particular overlay provides a better positioning with companies that have lower than average debt.

Finally, the **earnings per share (EPS)** and **PEG ratio** fields filter for stocks that show reasonable growth. The requirement to screen out those companies with PEG ratios above one and those that have P/E ratios above their projected EPS growth rates is very important. By doing so, it will be clear that the results will have analysts showing that they believe in the stock's prospect for growth and that most investors have not over exaggerated the buying. Therefore, the current price is in line or lower than it should be, taking into consideration earnings and earnings growth.

📖 EARNINGS PER SHARE (EPS)

This ratio is perhaps the most widely used by analysts because it reveals how much profit was gained on a per-share basis. On its own, EPS is not particularly useful. When sizing up the value of a company's stock using the EPS ratio, you must compare the current figure to that from the previous quarter or year. When doing so, you can properly determine the rate of growth for a company's earnings.

📖 PEG RATIO

This ratio represents a hybrid application of the P/E ratio (the price to earnings ratio—fully defined later in Chapter 4) and a company's annual growth rate. If a stock's PEG falls below a value of one, it is typically considered underpriced. If it jumps much higher than one, it is considered overpriced. It should be noted that when applied on its own, the accuracy of this formula has been questioned by many reputable economists.

Momentum Stocks

Trading on a short-term basis has provided both boom and bust outcomes for many. The theory of investing in stocks based on technical factors such as volume traded, comparative price changes, and recent price changes was, and is, the home for day traders.

Yet, with that said, it has to be understood that there are those who want *hot* stocks and lots of trading action for a portion of their portfolio. Still, whether or not you believe that this is a good investment strategy is another story altogether.

Screening can be used to find information about the underlying **technicals**📖 of a stock. A wonderful search that can be found directly on the *MSN Money* website looks for stocks whose prices have moved rapidly higher during the past six months. The screen also has requirement of at least a $100 million market cap and an average daily volume of at least 10,000, to help exclude very small companies.

📖 TECHNICALS

The trading patterns exhibited by a stock. For more information, see Chapter 3.

The primary result will be stocks with terrific performance over the past few weeks. It also searches for companies with increasing trading volume. Theoretically, the increased volume will lead us toward stocks that are finding more interest with investors.

Momentum Stocks

Fieldname	Operator	Value
Market Capitalization	>=	100,000,000
On Balance Volume	>=	80
On Balance Volume	<=	300
Average Daily Volume Last 2 Weeks	>=	Average Daily Volume Last Month
Average Daily Volume Last Month	>=	Average Daily Volume Last Quarter
Average Daily Volume Last Quarter	>=	Average Daily Volume Last Year
Average Daily Volume Last Month	>=	10,000
6-Month Relative Strength	>=	90
12-Month Relative Strength	>=	90
3-Month Relative Strength	>=	6-Month Relative Strength
% Price Change 1 Week	>=	5

As you look at the screening criteria for this search, notice how the progression starts from the most recent time period and extends forward. The next time period of volume is compared to the previous to ensure gains during the more recent period. Momentum is the goal here.

With that in mind, it is time to move on to the next topic in order to help bring some of this together. It is wise to remember that none of the disciplines that are presented represent a black-box answer to investment analysis. Only when combined with the appropriate investment research and analysis should a decision be reached to buy or sell a stock.

Use each of the disciplines as building blocks to gain insight into the future direction for your investments. Then develop a thorough understanding of the company, and the answers to the many questions you seek will become clear.

As you have seen, the application of hard numbers—if not simply the intricate formulas—plays a basic yet valuable role in a disciplined investment strategy. But, as mentioned near the end of Chapter 1, the numbers do not stop there. In the next chapter you will find a detailed account of the second component of our approach—technical analysis. It is a discipline that relies on three key premises to reveal a visual account of market movement: efficiency, history, and trends.

Chapter 3

Technical Analysis

There are three basic premises that **technical analysis**📖 is predicated upon: 1) markets have trends; 2) markets are efficient; and 3) history repeats itself. The latter is only true because people are creatures of habit. During your lifetime, you will tend to react to the same conditions in a similar fashion almost every time. Economist Harry S. Dent, Jr. has termed this "the human model of forecasting."

📖 TECHNICAL ANALYSIS
Technical analysis is the use of historical statistics of investment supply and demand to discover and exploit stock price patterns. This technique is not limited to stocks, but can also can be used to forecast market indices, industries, sectors, bonds, currencies, and commodities.

These actions and reactions translate to buy-and-sell events in the investment marketplace. They are then charted by a technical analyst who looks to uncover potential patterns and trends. Many patterns can be accurately measured and ultimately forecasted in order to determine cycle highs and lows, creating signals that determine when to get in or out of the market. Note that the previous sentence states that the *patterns* and not the forecasts can be accurately measured and ultimately forecasted. Forecasting where a particular stock or a market index is headed is not a clear-cut scientific process.

The technical analyst, also known as a technician, gauges how investors "feel" about a certain company by watching the flow of monies in and out of that particular stock. They do not concern themselves with profitability ratios, growth rates or product pipelines. That is the job of the fundamental analyst (see Chapter 4).

The technician believes that all of the known financial information pertaining to a stock is already priced into the market in the form of supply and demand (the **Efficient Market Theory**).

📖 EFFICIENT MARKET THEORY
This refers to the extent to which securities prices reflect what is known and promptly adjust to what becomes known. Even with the advent of technology, an active press, and easily accessible online trading, there is still an ongoing debate about market efficiency.

Those that subscribe to the efficient market theory argue that markets are properly priced, giving consideration to the point that all information available has been already discounted in the price. The implication is that there is nothing that will help an individual or an advisor consistently beat the markets.

Proponents of passive investment management, and specifically advocates of index investing, believe this theory and cling to any and all evidence they can conjure up. At the same time, it is difficult to disagree with the fact that most active money managers have a hard time outperforming their benchmark index on a regular basis.

The counter-group, of course, feels that this is just hogwash and contends that an investor, through research, can find stocks that will outperform the market. Warren Buffett and Peter Lynch are prime examples.

Since the market is an anticipatory mechanism, technicians can forecast changes in stock prices more quickly by looking at charts than the fundamentalist can by taking time to analyze a company's financial data. To illustrate this fact, think about how many times you have witnessed a stock rising or falling for no apparent reason. Then, after a fundamental change (earnings announcement) or newsworthy item (CEO retirement) is announced, the stock price starts to rise or fall once again. By the time you find out the specifics as to why the stock price has moved, it is usually too late.

This is where technical analysis can prove to be a beneficial tool. In essence, you can analyze and interpret charts in order to act on a stock movement without having to wait for the catalyst to appear. Keep in mind, however, that if there *are* significant financial concerns underlying the company, the chart may not be a particularly helpful tool. In fact, it can be quite harmful.

The most successful professional **day-traders** are, at the core, good technical analysts. Day-traders are frowned upon by many old-school money managers, but given today's stock market and its increased volatility, this type of trading has a tendency to be extremely profitable.

📖 DAY-TRADERS

A stock trader that falls within the category of "very active." The typical day-trader tends to hold stock positions for a relatively short time, opting instead to make multiple trades (sometimes dozens) on most days. These investors usually view stock trading as an independent career rather than a vehicle for amassing a retirement fund or generating supplemental income.

Day-traders are just one type of short-term trader. This group also contains swing-traders, market-timers, and many short-sellers. In today's market, a great deal of the daily market volatility can be attributed to their influences.

Think back. How many times have you seen top blue chip stocks come out with great earnings reports and subsequently watched their share prices drop like rocks?

There are two reasons for this. First, investors are always trying to get in or out before everyone else does. The strategy for trigger-happy investors is to buy on the rumor and then sell on the fact, or vice versa. Therefore, if the consensus believes that a certain stock will hit or surpass its expected quarterly earnings, investors will begin to bid up that stock ahead of the earnings release. Then, when the good *or* bad news is announced, the short-term traders of the world start selling, taking out the profits they made on the way up. If the stock moves against them, they will also sell in an attempt to limit their losses.

Second, using technical analysis will tip off the day-trader as to the sentiment surrounding the stock. Money flow into the stock grows on higher volume, telling the short-term trader that the fundamentals are looking bullish, signaling a potential buying opportunity. When money flow into the stock drops off, the amount of buyers and sellers is, in effect, balancing out. This, in turn, translates into a stock that is only fairly valued to investors. At this point, the short-term trader sees no further price appreciation and dumps the position, causing the stock to fall.

The most prudent of the new breed of *Disciplined Investors* will not confine his or her investment strategy to charting alone. The optimal strategy combines both fundamental and technical analysis skills to create a disciplined investment style for long-term wealth accumulation. A fundamental (financial) review should uncover the strengths and weaknesses of a firm. Then, if the stock is fundamentally sound, technical analysis can be implemented to make an informed decision on when to buy into or sell out of the position.

Chart Analysis

A technician needs to be able to analyze many different types of charts. First though, they need to understand the principles of how charts are constructed and what each piece of information represents.

(Data Source: Yahoo! Finance)

For our purposes, a bar chart will be used as a starting point. Below is a sample of a daily bar chart showing the high, low, and close data points (HLC).

Chart Components

On the left/vertical axis of the chart above, you will find the stock price of IBM. On the top/horizontal axis is the date range. For every date, you will find a corresponding data point. From these points, you can find the opening and closing prices, the high for the day, and the low for the day. In addition, for each day, you can easily see the full price range of executed trades.

An example of a data point:

Take a closer look at the data point:

The "trading range" refers to the range of prices the stock was selling at throughout the day. The top of the trading range is the highest price at which the stock was sold and the bottom of the range is the lowest price at which the stock was traded. The closing price is how the stock ended at the end of the trading day.

To determine the opening price, simply refer to the previous day's data point and find the closing price. That closing price is usually the opening price for the next trading day.

There can be much more information included on a stock chart, some of which will be addressed later in this chapter. This important additional information includes studies such as volume, moving averages, oscillator lines, and the MACD (pronounced Mac-dee) indicator.

Now that you better understand the basic components of a basic stock chart, the analysis of various price patterns will be easy to comprehend.

Time Period
Before further exploring the components that make up a technical chart, one point needs to be made clear: technical analysts look at price charts constructed over any length of time, including yearly, monthly, daily, intra-day, and even tick-by-tick. You will see a data point corresponding to each and every **trading period**. 📖

📖 TRADING PERIOD
The last point in a given time period in which trade prices are reported. If the chart is made up of daily pricing, the end-of-day price will be one of the data points. The high or low may also be included, depending on the chart type.

Price Patterns

First, and perhaps the most obvious, is the fact that stock prices can only move in three directions: up, down, and sideways. Price patterns can get very detailed and complex; so much so that any number of books could have been (and have been) written on price patterns alone.

This section will illustrate various price patterns in order to provide you with a base of knowledge, helping you to recognize the most popular patterns that technical analysts use. Keep in mind that the overall objective is to help you profit from stock investments.

Trading in a Range

As discussed previously, stock prices are fueled by human expectations and therefore, recognizable cycles will often emerge. These usually consist of peaks (highs) and valleys (lows).

The following illustration is a simplified example of a "cyclical trend." The assumption is that humans have varying perspectives. At the same time, they generally predict that cycles will usually continue to trend in the same manner over and over. Remember, these cycles can occur over any period of time, no matter how long or short.

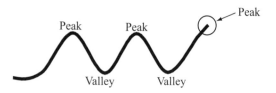

The trend, illustrated above, is at a peak as related to its historical performance or pattern. This does not necessarily mean that the price will move lower in the future, just because the pattern has done that before. Nor does it mean that the price will continue climbing higher.

From the viewpoint of an investor and specifically a technical analyst, this is not the most opportune time to buy. Rather, this pattern is seen as a bearish indicator (negative sentiment) and signals a good time to sell, or could indicate a short-sale opportunity. The opposite would be true if the trend line were in or near the valley. At that point, it would probably represent a buying opportunity. Therefore, cyclical trend lines are not strong buy or sell indicators.

Consolidation

Consolidation (illustrated below), or "formation of a rectangle" (shown by lines A and B), occurs when pressure is building up in a stock. A consolidation phase is usually a temporary stall in a pattern. The belief is that if a stock has been in an uptrend and then begins to consolidate, the prevailing uptrend should continue and a breakout through the resistance level will soon follow.

This assumption can be made unless the price breaks through the support level, signaling the confirmation of a reversal of the previous trend. This consolidation rectangle can provide strong evidence of future direction:

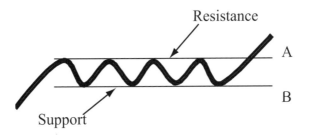

Congestion

A stock is in a "congestion phase" (example below) when there are no obvious patterns emerging. Along with this type of trend comes indecisiveness with regard to technical direction. This usually indicates confusion about the underlying direction of the stock on the part of investors.

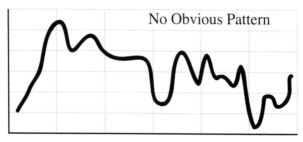

A stock trading in this manner will not attract the technical analyst, as there are no definitive price patterns signaling any action.

Upward Trend

An "upward trend" occurs when a stock begins to move higher. In the situation illustrated below, each successive high becomes higher than the last and each successive low is also higher than the last. An upward trend is a bullish indicator that signals a buying opportunity, as a stock may be breaking out through its resistance levels and beyond.

(Source: MSN Money)

Downward Trend

A "downward trend" is the exact opposite of an upward trend. Each successive high is lower than the last and each successive low is also lower. This will often signal a sell, as the stock price may be falling below support levels and may be carrying a negative sentiment regarding its underlying fundamentals.

(Source: MSN Money)

Resistance and Support

A "resistance level" can be defined as a ceiling (high-end), perhaps as the result of purchases made before a decline. The general thinking is that investors, waiting for a rebound, will seek to sell when the stock price has recovered enough to wipe out their losses. Thus, the stock or the market as a whole is prevented from moving higher.

On the other side, the "support level" is the price point at which investors seem comfortable to buy (the low-end), perhaps because it is as low as the stock seems to be going, or because the apparent bargain becomes irresistible. The trading range between the support level and resistance level is known as a "channel." Look at the chart, on the next page, for Texas Utilities (TXU) and notice the channel between the resistance level of $42.50 and the support level of $39.00.

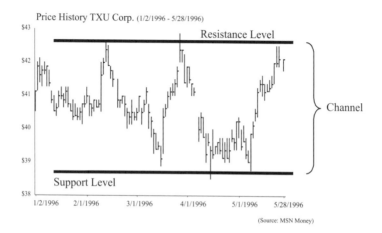

Price History TXU Corp. (1/2/1996 - 5/28/1996)

(Source: MSN Money)

In order to become a significant support or resistance price, the chart should show several successive and unsuccessful attempts to breach a price level. When you attempt to draw either, look to a chart that shows a significant number of periods to allow for an accurate representation of the price activity.

As stated before, stock prices can only go in three directions: up, down, and sideways. The chart of Texas Utilities (above) is an illustration of a sideways trend, which usually follows and precedes an upward or downward trend.

Now, look at the second Texas Utilities chart, located on the bottom of the following page. Notice the downward trend, illustrating the market is turning in favor of the sellers—in other words, the trend is moving toward more sellers of the stock than buyers.

In the first consolidation phase (number one), there is a leveling out of the stock price as buyers and sellers begin to even out. As this sideways trend continues, there is a buildup of pressure in the stock, and eventually there will be either a reversal or a continuation of the previous downward trend.

You can anticipate this next trend by looking at the resistance and support levels. In the first sideways trend (1), notice the resistance at about $48.00 per share and the support holds at around $47.75 per share (a very tight channel). Once the price dips below support, it indicates a confirmation signal. It did just that on September 20th of that year and provided the technical analyst the ability to forecast a continuation of the previous downward trend. The result would probably be a sale of a long position or an initiation of a short-sale.

In the example, the trend continues downward to just under $46 per share and the next or secondary consolidation phase begins (2). If, instead, the stock price breaks out above the support level, it could indicate a buying opportunity.

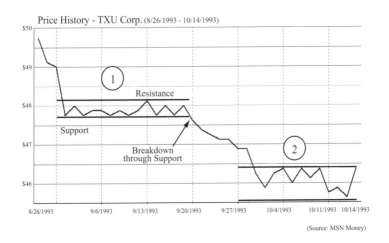

Price History - TXU Corp. (8/26/1993 - 10/14/1993)

(Source: MSN Money)

Discovering these consolidation phases can be very helpful for taking advantage of swings in stock prices for a daily momentum trade, or when looking for the optimal price or time to enter a stock transaction. Bear in mind, though, that many times when a price breaks out or falls through there is the chance that it represents a "fake out" and the price may boomerang back. Therefore it is recommended to wait for the price to surpass at least three percent over the resistance *or* three percent under the support price before assuming the confirmation signal is accurate.

Head and Shoulders

Another popular (and perhaps the most reliable) price pattern is the "head and shoulders distribution" as shown below. The pattern consists of three separate and distinct rallies. One rally (the head) is sandwiched between two smaller rallies. The first shoulder is the initial run in the bull rally and the second shoulder is basically the start of a bearish decline.

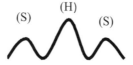

A very important aspect of any price pattern is the technical indicators that accompany them. Look at the chart below and take notice of the daily prices of Sample Stock, Inc. and the volume illustrated by the vertical bars at the bottom.

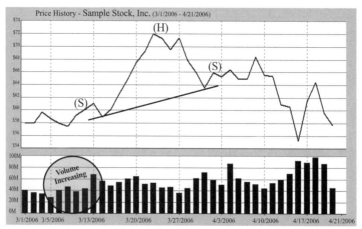

(Source: Horowitz & Company)

Trading activity is usually heavier during the formation of the first shoulder, as can be seen by the volume indicator related to that period. The confirmation (or the development of a head and shoulders pattern) is signaled during the formation of the second shoulder.

The head and shoulders pattern does not always need to have a symmetrical look to it. Rather, it may come in many different shapes and sizes as shown here:

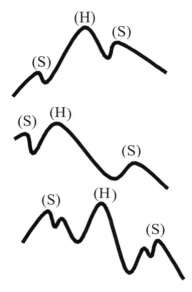

If the pattern is flipped, or the head forms a bottom (see below), it is known as an inverted head and shoulders pattern, which is actually a bullish indicator.

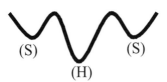

When presented with a head and shoulders pattern, you can often measure the expected price movement up or down during the pattern's lifecycle. Refer to the chart depicting the NASDAQ Composite Index during 2000, shown below. By drawing a straight line connecting the low points (shoulders) on each side of the head, you have easily created a "neckline."

Next, draw a line from the highest point on the head to the neckline. Then, take that distance (sometimes referred to as the range) and subtract it from the neckline. This is the estimated level to which the price can theoretically fall.

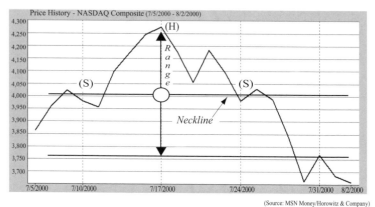

(Source: MSN Money/Horowitz & Company)

In addition, the period of time it takes for the head and shoulders pattern to develop is usually a good indicator of how long or short the correction could last. Therefore, if you notice a head and shoulders pattern that developed over a two-year period, you could expect a potentially lengthy correction on the other end of the pattern.

In the summer of 2000, the downside range from this pattern became a short-term resistance level as investors were looking for direction. At the end of July 2000, the stock market continued to slide and buyers began to step in, hoping that the end of the correction was near.

Those buyers assumed that the drop below the neckline range created an oversold situation. They bid the market up to the resistance level, which at one time was support. Once they realized that there was a price ceiling and that the bounce was not going to move beyond that level, selling ensued once again.

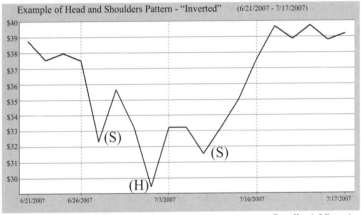

(Source: Horowitz & Company)

Double Top and Double Bottom

The "double top" is a major reversal pattern that usually emerges after an upward trend has occurred. As you would expect, the pattern consists of two significant tops or heads. It usually precedes a bearish move and sometimes even market corrections as well. One important note about double tops is that they are typically confirmed if they are separated by 30 or more periods.

If there is no clear confirmation of the pattern, it may actually be a normal resistance level that will eventually break. The time requirement helps to separate the real pattern from a fake-out. Another signal that will help with confirmation of this pattern is the occurrence of accelerating volume as the price declines. If you notice the lowest level between the tops has been breached on increasing volume, this usually represents a clear sell signal.

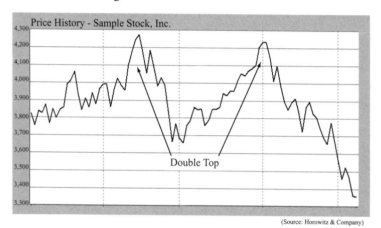

(Source: Horowitz & Company)

The "double bottom" is really the opposite of the double top in that it usually signals a forthcoming rally. If you think about it for a moment, both of these indicators are simply showing technical investors that there is a price level that has not been breached. It shows either a support or resistance point

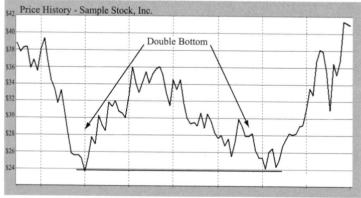

(Source: Horowitz & Company)

that has been well established. In this pattern, there have been multiple times when key levels have been reached but not broken. The forecast will usually predict that the trend should hold the support (bullish) or be limited by the resistance (bearish).

All of the material presented in this chapter merely scrapes the surface. This tip of the iceberg presentation is intended to be a primer to introduce you to the valid approaches used in technical analysis that are at your disposal. By mastering the forms of research explained within these pages, you will be well on your way to becoming a self-driven investor with a keen sense of discipline—and with this newfound knowledge can come steady and stable growth for your portfolio.

As with anything, history has a great deal to teach us. The investment markets are often cyclical and usually have a way of creating repetitive patterns. With a sharp eye to what has already been revealed, you can shrewdly carve out a path toward a successful investing experience.

There are times when charting, on its own, falls short as a means of projecting outcomes for the market. Fortunately there are other forms of analysis that will allow you to take a look at a company's public records in order to gain a clearer picture of the here-and-now of a stock's growth potential.

In the following chapter, you will find an overview of this process—the discipline known as fundamental analysis. It is much different from what has been discussed so far. What you will find is that a fundamental analyst tries to anticipate the rate of growth of a firm's earnings and uses other ratios to predict a stock's price. Essentially, the research is used to determine if a stock is over- or undervalued and then invest accordingly.

Chapter 4

Fundamental Analysis

Thousands of people around the world make their livings by analyzing securities. This is a relatively new vocation, as it was only around the turn of the last century that buying and selling stocks became honorable. Once it began to gain a better reputation, it caused many of the speculators to leave the market in search of the next unsavory opportunity. Prior to the stock market as we know it today, people utilized the markets as more of a center for legal gambling than a place for long-term growth.

Many of today's analysts work for institutional money managers such as mutual funds, pension funds, and insurance companies. They are often labeled as "buy-side" analysts because they are looking to buy or sell securities specifically on behalf of the firms they work for. Their analysis and reviews need to be unbiased and accurate in order to ensure that the firms will make well-informed decisions concerning their expectations for profitable opportunities.

The remainder of the practitioners are considered "sell-side" since their purpose is to create reports that will entice investors to purchase a particular stock. This faction works largely for brokerage houses and securities firms.

The average investor can easily obtain the advice presented by the latter crowd, since they are in the business of generating fees from transactions. Because of this, hundreds of reports are authored every day. Consequently, as a *Disciplined Investor*, you need to take extra care when reviewing price targets and recommendations found in reports that may be overly optimistic.

📖   FUNDAMENTAL ANALYSIS

A method wherein an investor searches for winning stocks by researching a company's earnings history, balance sheet, management, product line, and other factors that will affect its profitability and growth. The significant difference in fundamental analysis versus technical analysis is that the fundamental analyst will look at information pertaining to a company's finances that are obtained from their annual statements as well as news items. Past trading patterns are of no concern, as the focus is on the future. They seek out companies that will have financial and business catalysts to help improve their shareholder value. This discipline is considerably more "long-term" minded.

The art of creating a stock report is at the center of the fundamental analysts' daily routine. They do this in an effort to fully understand the current financial health of a company and to make educated buy, sell, or hold decisions.

As a *Disciplined Investor* on your way to learning the inner workings of fundamental analysis, you will need to rely on information and data that is current and accurate. In addition, historical data and future projections are vital tools in this process. Since the market is very efficient, the slightest miscalculation or the use of incorrect data could cause devastating financial results.

History has vividly shown to us many times over that stocks can literally be *crushed* by the announcement of an accounting change or a restatement of earnings. With this in mind, it is a non-negotiable prerequisite that as you make your analysis you look for reliable sources of information for the raw data.

Similarly, it is essential that you understand the equations behind the various ratios that you use. Question and re-question the information. Is the ratio developed using past or future earnings? Do you have accurate and up-to-date information from the balance sheet and income statements? Are the figures you are using adjusted for splits and dividends? These are just some of the questions that will be answered in this chapter.

Volumes upon volumes have been written on this very subject, and this chapter will attempt to convey it in only a few pages. Realize that this is intended to be an overview and guide on how to properly utilize the most important techniques and latest systems developed for the disciplined investor. Some will be taken from investment icons like Benjamin Graham, Jeremy Siegel, and David Dodd, as well as other well-known and well-respected experts in the field.

Ultimately, upon completing this chapter, you will have all the tools necessary to help you understand the inner dynamics of fundamental analysis. This will provide you with a major advantage over your neighbors in properly interpreting information and financial statements.

When you begin to analyze a company, there are a few basic items that need to be understood. The "must list" consists of a review of the company in question, its business proceedings, present and historical earnings, analyst recommendations, financial projections, and price targets. Additionally, a thorough review of recent research reports should be completed in order to provide you with a multidimensional picture of the company. This will eventually assist you during the final process of an informed buy or sell decision.

Too many times, hearsay and tips are used as "sound financial investigation" only to turn out to be a big monetary bust (tax losses are available as a small consolation).

Finally, it needs to be said that the use of this technique is not rigid. Many derivations of the basic principals have been used over the years in an attempt to find the magic formula. You should embrace the idea of working within the framework, but do it with flexibility.

Search outside the box to discover alternative ways of applying the data. Remember that when it comes to the market, there are no absolute answers, so you do not have to restrict your thoughts to the teachings of others. Rather, use them for guidance when forming general parameters and in the creation of your own unique disciplines.

The best way to start off is with a few important definitions. These will be used throughout this and other chapters, so it is wise to become familiar with them, as they are the "talk of the street." When investors chatter, this basic vernacular is the lingo of money.

Financial Statement and Ratio Analysis

Income Statements

Income statements reveal how much revenue a company brings into the business by providing services and/or goods to its customers over a specific timeframe. It is intended to show the costs and expenses related to procuring the revenue acquired during the specified time.

The income statement also shows two main categories of information for each period covered. First is the revenue from products and services that the company has sold. Next are the expenses—the actual costs of doing business. Analysts pay close attention to this statement and rely upon information related to revenue, gross profit, operating income, net earnings, and earnings per share when interpreting a company's financial position.

Revenue

Revenue can be earned by companies in many ways. They can sell products and services or possibly lease or rent equipment. They can also earn dividends and interest on loans they supply to other companies. Many companies have several sources of revenue while others rely on a single stream of income. As an example, a company such as Apple may receive income from selling products as well as manufacturing. They may also receive a commission from selling music and books. They could report revenues from consulting and services, which may additionally include rentals, financing, and maintenance. In addition, they may earn dividends and capital gains on various investments that will also be included as revenue.

Gross Profit

You are undoubtedly familiar with the belief that if you want to make money, you usually have to spend money. For most companies, the cost of goods sold (COGS), also know as the cost of sales, is the greatest cost of generating revenue.

For example, Dell Computers must buy circuit boards and semiconductors to make its computers. They also have to pay their workers and management teams as well as spend money on property expenses, power, and maintenance. All of these expenses are deducted from the revenue, leaving the company's gross profit (net revenue minus cost of sales = gross profit).

As stated above, the cost of goods sold is usually the greatest cost for any business. A company that manufactures and sells *products* will usually have a higher level of expenses related to COGS, while a company that provides mainly *services* will have a higher level of salaries, bonuses, and benefits.

Operating Income

Beyond the expenses directly related to manufacturing a product, you will find operating expenses. Spending that falls under this category could include items such as salaries for office staff, research and development costs, advertising costs related to the sale of the product or service, and other administrative costs. When these are subtracted from the gross profit, the number that remains is considered the operating income or loss.

Launching a new product or service or attempting a physical expansion will cause most companies to carry operating expenses that are much higher than normal. Attention to detail in this area should be maintained to fully understand why the operating expenses have increased on a year-over-year basis in order to properly project future operating income.

Some firms may incur large expenses as they expand in an attempt to gain market share. As you look through the income statement, try to identify and make note of the annual changes on a separate piece of paper. As you build your list of items to be reviewed further, you will start to develop a virtual picture of what has really happened within the company over time.

Additional questions may come up and can be answered after a further review of the annual report or by calling the company directly. Shareholder service representatives are usually more than happy to help with basic requests regarding reported operations.

It may be a good idea to call the direct line of a company that you are considering investing in. You can usually call a company's investor relations department and speak to a knowledgeable source that should be able to provide accurate information regarding the company.

Here is a real example of this idea in action: a number of years ago, an investor was searching for additional information on Tosco, a company in the oil sector. It was 8:00 a.m., and there was a need for additional information to clarify a few discrepancies about their inventories.

The decision was made to call the direct line and ask to speak to the chief financial officer. Amazingly, he picked up the phone himself. It was early in the morning and apparently his assistant had not yet arrived to screen his calls. After a 10-minute conversation, the investor had all of the information he needed to make an important financial decision. The clarification helped to explain the issue and in the end the transaction was highly profitable.

Net Earnings
The "bottom line" is by far the most important item in any financial analysis. This often-used phrase may quite possibly be derived from the fact that there is actually a "last line" on financial statements.

Once the deductions are subtracted from the gross revenue, the result is considered to be the net earnings (or loss). If the company had a good year and their expenses were less than their revenue, they would (or at least should) show a profit. On the other hand, if the contrary is true, the cash flow statement will show a loss.

During the latter part of the 90s, many "dot-com" companies were surviving on money in the bank in an attempt to capitalize on future technology promised by the new millennium. This is precisely why most now refer to many of those companies as "dot-bombs." It was a folly for them to spend down their primary sources of capitalization rather than actively seek profitable business models that would provide for their income needs.

When a company has negative earnings is a good indication of what lies ahead. There is no possible way that any business can maintain viability when it is continually showing a net loss. Case in point: the staggering number of bankruptcies that plagued the business-to-consumer market of the "dot-com" industry at the turn of the century.

With that in mind, there is still the potential for a company to make a turnaround and become highly profitable, even if it is currently showing a loss. Be certain that there is substantial evidence that there is or will be a catalyst that will help to turn the loss into a gain. Otherwise, there will surely come a time when the company will need to stop the bleeding. If it gets to that point, you will wish you were never a shareholder.

Earnings Per Share (EPS)
Earnings per share is the best means of understanding the profitability of a company. It is the net earnings or income of the company divided by the number of shares outstanding. This particular number can be used as a base to calculate many other useful comparative ratios.

$$EPS = Net\ Income \div Shares\ Outstanding$$

Suppose that a company has 2,000,000 shares outstanding and earns $4,000,000 per year. Since the EPS is a division of the two, the result will be $2 of EPS per share. This simple ratio is one of the core principles in analyzing the fundamentals of a stock. It helps to show the relative earnings of a stock when compared to others in the same industry.

Earnings are by far the most important component when calculating the true value of the stock. Whether a multiple is applied or a discounted calculation is used, this is probably the one instrument that most analysts include in their studies. The good news is that historical earnings information is easy to come by. The bad news is that estimates of future earnings are known to have wide ranges with limited accuracy.

Even companies that make their livings "guesstimating" future earnings have acknowledged their relative inabilities to properly forecast the future. Moreover, the greater the distance from today until the actual earnings report, the more deviated the estimated earnings are likely to be from the actual result.

Price-to-Earnings Ratio

The most commonly used ratio is probably the price-to-earnings (P/E) ratio. This is sometimes referred to as the "price multiple" or "earnings multiple."

To calculate this ratio, you take the closing price and divide it by the earnings per share (EPS) for the previous 12 months. This ratio helps one to understand whether or not a stock is over- or under-valued.

> Current P/E Ratio = Price ÷ Current Earnings
> Forward P/E Ratio = Price ÷ Estimated Earnings
> Trailing P/E Ratio = Price ÷ Prior Earnings

When looking at this ratio, it is important not to view it in a vacuum. This is one of those ratios that should be used in a comparison, rather than on a stand-alone basis. Every market sector has a different P/E in which its members can be compared. Make sure to look at this ratio with that in mind. Be careful not to compare the P/E of significantly different industries such as a technology company and a bank since it will have no relevance. Technology, health care, biotech, and some service companies often trade at P/Es above 40, or about double the average of the stocks comprising the S&P 500 index. Financials, utilities, and certain **old economy stocks**📖 typically have below-market P/E ratios.

📖   OLD ECONOMY STOCKS
A term used to describe the old "blue chip" industries and
stocks that enjoyed fabulous growth during the early parts of
the 20th century. These companies are usually very
traditional in their ways of doing business. Industries such as
energy, steel, and autos are considered to be members of the
old economy.

Often times, a high P/E ratio is reflective of soaring expectations that investors have for a stock. Think about this: Who
would invest in anything that would require them to wait 20 or
40 years to make back their original money?

Here is a another way of looking at it: When you invest
in high P/E stocks, the expectation is that future earnings
will grow. In other words, if a company has a forward P/E of
40, it means that the stock price is 40 times the earnings per
share. Or, said another way, the company's value is 40 times
its earnings.

If that were equated to a simple investment, it would show
that for each $100,000 you would earn only $2,500 per year.
Consider the fact that an elevated P/E ratio may also be reflective of poor earnings. Similarly, a lower ratio may signify
negative investor expectations, an undervalued stock, or both.

Imagine that you had a dime that was brand new. It was
rare, it had a limited-edition stamp on the back, and you
preserved it well. You could say that the raw value of the coin
was $0.10.

Now imagine that someone you knew was willing to buy
it for $1.00. Essentially, they were willing to spend $0.90 more

due to the quality and rarity of the coin. They most likely wanted to enter into the transaction because they believed that the dime would be worth more in the future and they would be able to sell it for a profit. In the language of the markets, the coin was selling at a price multiple of 10 or a P/E of 10.

Price Multiple of Coin = Trading Value ÷ Coin Value

Hence: Price Multiple of Coin = $1.00 ÷ $0.10 = 10

Apply this example to a publicly traded security using the same basic math. If you know the earnings of a company and the current market price per share, you can easily calculate the P/E ratio.

Here are a few *historical* examples of stocks and sample P/E ratio calculations:

Company Name	Price per Share	EPS	P/E Ratio
Abercrombie & Fitch	$ 67.25	$ 4.23	15.90
Apple	$ 88.35	$ 2.27	38.92
Boeing	$ 89.80	$ 2.12	42.36
Dell	$ 26.35	$ 1.23	21.42
Microsoft	$ 28.90	$ 1.26	22.94
Proctor & Gamble	$ 63.90	$ 2.66	24.02
Wal-Mart	$ 46.42	$ 2.62	17.72

To level the field, an excellent derivation of the P/E ratio is used to see if a stock is valued fairly compared to its own future growth. This is called the **PEG ratio** or price-to-earnings-to-growth ratio.

📖   PEG RATIO

The calculation: price/earnings (P/E) ratio *divided by* expected per-share earnings growth over the next year. More than likely, a result that is less than one tells us that we may have a good investment that is undervalued for the time being. On the other hand, a result of more than one is usually a sign that the position is valued higher than it should be.

Originally, the PEG Ratio was developed to look at stock statistics in more than one dimension. By adding expected growth to the P/E ratio, it will effectively provide a comparison tool to level the playing field when valuing stocks.

Small- to mid-cap stocks are well suited to utilize the PEG Ratio as the initial screening tool since they usually pay little or no dividends. In effect, it is a good tool for some stocks that are usually more difficult to value using traditional methods.

Just as it is true that the ratio is beneficial for smaller stocks, larger stocks should have an additional requirement to help create a more useable and appropriate valuation tool. By simply adding an overlay of dividend yield along with the earnings a much better outcome can be crafted for large-cap stocks.

PEG ratios are considered less useful in assessing cyclical stocks and those in the banking, oil, or real estate industries, where assets are more accurate indicators of relative value. With these stocks, the growth rates are low and the company's assets are a much better indicator of stock value.

PEG Ratio	Signal
.50 or less	Strong Buy
.50 to .75	Buy
.75 to 1.00	Hold
1.00 to 1.25	Possible Sell
1.25 to 1.75	Consider Shorting
Over 1.75	Short/Sell

PEG is probably one of the best fundamental tools to use in assessing the optimal time to enter or exit a stock position. The discipline will allow you to take some of the emotion out of the buy-and-sell decision so that you will not get caught up in the average investor's predicament of latching on to a favorite stock and never letting go. As they say, "It's not the buy strategy that makes a successful investor; it's the sell strategy." Remember, no one ever went bankrupt by taking a profit.

Balance Sheet Ratios
There are those stocks for which earnings are of less importance than their assets. This is a notable distinction, given that not every company does the same thing. Therefore, you should use a separate set of valuation techniques, depending on the exact type of company.

As has been explained via the PEG ratio, it is appropriate to approach some sectors in a different manner than you might approach others, depending on the way companies within the given sector do business. Stocks within the cyclical, financial, utility, and defense sectors can be better assessed from the values of the holdings than from the revenues they make from their ventures.

Sample Income Statement for IBM

Annual Income Statement (in millions)	Year 5	Year 4	Year 3	Year 2	Year 1
Net Sales	$87,548	$81,667	$78,508	$75,947	$71,940
Cost of Sales	49,034	45,803	42,898	40,396	35,971
Gross Profit	38,514	35,864	35,610	35,551	35,969
Selling, General & Administrative Expense	20,002	21,708	21,511	21,943	22,776
EBITDA	18,512	14,156	14,099	13,608	13,193
Depreciation & Amortization	6,585	4,992	5,001	5,012	5,602
EBIT	11,927	9,164	9,098	8,596	7,591
Other Income, Net	557	589	657	707	947
Income before Income Expense	12,484	9,753	9,755	9,303	8,538
Interest Expense	727	713	728	716	725
Income before Taxes	11,757	9,040	9,027	8,587	7,813
Income Taxes	4,045	2,712	2,934	3,158	3,635
Special Income/Charges	0	0	0	0	0
Net Income from Continuing Operations	7,712	6,328	6,093	5,429	4,178
Net Income from Discontinued Operations	0	0	0	0	0
Net Income from Total Operations	7,712	6,328	6,093	5,429	4,178

Continued...

Annual Income Statement (in millions)	Year 5	Year 4	Year 3	Year 2	Year 1
Normalized Income	$7,712	$6,328	$6,093	$5,429	$4,178
Extraordinary Income	0	0	0	0	0
Income from Cumulative Effect of Accounting Changes	0	0	0	0	0
Income from Tax Loss Carry-forward	0	0	0	0	0
Other Gains (Losses)	0	0	0	0	0
Total Net Income	7,712	6,328	6,093	5,429	4,178
Dividends Paid per Share	0.41	0.43	0.39	0.33	0.25
Preferred Dividends	0.20	0.20	0.20	0.20	0.62
Earnings per Share	2.24	2.12	1.87	1.75	1.59

Sample data for illustrative purposes only.

This does not imply that you should take the income component and throw it out the window. It simply means that in the ultimate scheme of things, an analysis that looks at **balance sheet**⌨ items instead of the components contained in the income statement can be more effective for these groups.

📖 BALANCE SHEET

A firm's balance sheet (sometimes referred to as a "Statement of Financial Position") is a snapshot of its financial picture for a given moment in time. On the left side of the statement, companies detail their assets. The topmost position contains those assets with the greatest degree of liquidity, and as you move down they become less liquid.

On the right side are the liabilities (also known as the company's debt).The time order when payments are due is also shown from top to bottom. When liabilities are added to shareholder's equity, the result should equal the total value of assets.

By becoming familiar with the balance sheet, you will be able to skillfully analyze areas such as current assets and current liabilities. You can also compare a company's **liabilities**▭ to its shareholder's equity to find out more about the financial strength and amount of leverage a company has. This should help you decide whether the **assets**▭ have additional value beyond what is plainly visible on the statement.

Assets = Liabilities + Shareholder's Equity

▭   ASSETS
Simply put, assets are any item of value owned by a business. On the balance sheet a firm lists its assets, which are eventually reduced by its liabilities.

There are several types of assets a company can own. Each business is different but all will have some combination of capital stock, land (or some other form of real estate), inventory, trucks, and many other items of value. These assets will have differing abilities to create profits as well as differing levels of liquidity. Some assets are characterized as *tangible* while others may be considered *use* or even *current*.

As an example, inventory is usually very easy to convert to cash. Therefore it would be considered liquid. On the other end of the spectrum would be farmland and any other items that generally require a longer time to sell and, therefore, require much more time to liquidate. On the balance sheets, liquidity is important. It is differentiated by the terms *current assets* and *non-current assets*.

Another distinction is whether they are "real." Remember that some assets, such as cash, are easily valued and liquidated. Then there are those that are much more difficult to pin a price on, such as farmland and buildings. Regardless, the fact is that you can actually touch and feel these, and they are therefore considered "tangible assets."

Beyond those assets that we can easily see are those that have significant value but are not quite as apparent. Goodwill, as an example, may include the value of a name brand or possibly a well-known company spokesperson. (Think of William Shatner and Priceline.com.)

It takes a good eye to recognize the hidden values that may be found on the balance sheet. Consider Sears, for instance. For years, they were valued according to generally accepted accounting principles (GAAP) as well as traditional investment valuation techniques. It was only recently that the idea of valuing Sears to include their significant real estate holdings was introduced. This occurred as analysts realized that they have tremendous unrealized value in their land holdings. During 2004-2006, Sears' stock shot up as investors wanted to own them as a real estate play, in addition to their ability to create revenue from the sale of washers and dryers.

📖 LIABILITIES

The best way to look at these is to think about a traditional house that you may live in. The house has value (assets) and there is often a mortgage (liability). The liability that a company may have comes in the form of obligations to pay bills as well as the interest and principal payments on bonds.

Invariably, companies have liabilities. It is the nature of business to leverage funds to help with the day-to-day operations and ongoing expansion of the business. A few examples of a liability are taxes payable, payroll, rent, employee benefits, and services.

If a company is unable to make interest payments in a timely fashion during the repayment of a loan, their alternatives may include bankruptcy, reorganization, or absolute disbandment. Obviously, any of these would represent a problem. Therefore, as an investor, it is crucial to review the short- and long-term liabilities of a company on an ongoing basis.

When looking at the balance sheet, there are a few very interesting morsels of information that you can collect. First, you can find out how the company is capitalized. In other words, do they have more debt than cash, how much treasury stock do they own, and how much debt is outstanding? These are all important to uncover because they point to whether the company in question has sufficient backing to persevere in difficult times.

Companies that have high debt ratios are more apt to come under severe pressure in an increasing interest rate environment. Others that have a high amount of cash may be in very good positions to participate in profitable buyouts and mergers. One particular ratio that gets right to the heart of this matter is the **debt/equity ratio.**

> 📖 **DEBT/EQUITY RATIO**
> Taking the most recent quarter's long-term debt and dividing it by the most recent quarter's common stock equity is the basic method of calculation. Essentially, the debt/equity ratio is a calculation of the degree to which a company's capital has been used as compared to leverage.

Companies that are on an aggressive expansion plan are usually more leveraged than those that are stable and mature. In practice, the more leverage a company employs to help create profits, the greater the profit potential to the investor. This comes with a warning as well: leverage increases risk in proportion to the amount of potential gain.

Investors allow more conservative and stable companies (or companies that must adhere to stringent debt regulations) to have a greater level of debt, as it is presumed that their markets are more dependable. Food makers and oil companies are good examples of this.

Debt/Equity Ratio = Total Liabilities ÷ Shareholders Equity

Another test for information on the balance sheet is finding out whether the company in question has enough short-term assets to cover its immediate liabilities. This is important because as bills come in, the company will be required to make payment in a timely fashion. The "Quick Ratio," sometimes referred to as the "acid test," is an excellent method to examine the health of a company's debt.

Quick Ratio Calculation

$$\frac{(\text{Cash} + \text{Accounts Receivable} + \text{Short-term Investments})}{\text{Current Liabilities}}$$

An excellent tool used by value-oriented investors is the **price-to-book ratio**. This helps an investor know if the stock is trading at a premium or a discount when compared to the actual worth of the company. It effectively shows how much the company would be worth if it was forced to close its doors and liquidate. When the ratio is below one, bargain hunters find it to be an irresistible opportunity. Since we have seen that balance sheets will usually err on the side of a more conservative valuation, the company may be more overvalued than is reflected by a low price-to-book ratio.

> 📖 PRICE-TO-BOOK RATIO
>
> To calculate this ratio, use the latest price of the stock and divide it by the most recent quarter's book value per share. (Remember, book value is simply assets minus liabilities.) This is also known as the price/equity ratio.

It is a good idea to think about this ratio as the failsafe for ownership in a stock. The book value is at least the "ownership" value of the company for the stockholder. If the price moves below this, there is a good chance that investors will still retain some value. (Although there are those odd cases that will leave an investor with little more than a piece of paper as the value of their investment.)

Given all this, a very low price-to-book ratio makes some fundamental investors feel that a company has the ability to generate earnings and the opportunity for long-term profits.

This ratio, as with others, will be quite different for each industry. For some companies the price/book will be very useful (such as banks) and for others (such as biotechs) it will not.

Texas Utilities was chosen as an example of a company that may be better reviewed by the balance sheet and its related ratios. *MSN Money* has all of the latest raw data available—free—for you to do the same.

Expect most companies to do their best to focus their attention on assets, rather than liabilities. Be on the lookout for hidden items in the footnotes, especially with regard to liabilities. Make sure to have all information at hand to calculate the correct ratios and assumptions in order to create a good strategy. All of this will once again result in a well-informed and disciplined investment decision.

Do not worry if you do not master this exercise immediately. With practice, your eyes will become focused on the most important areas which will eventually allow for you to zero in on only the important items.

By looking at an annual comparison for Texas Utilities—between years 1 and 5—you are able to make a few observations. At first, it seems that the company has done an excellent job of increasing current assets. A move from a level of $848m in Year 1 to over $3,900m in Year 5 is a substantial increase.

Sample Balance Sheet for Texas Utilities

Annual Balance Sheet	Year 5	Year 4	Year 3	Year 2	Year 1
Assets					
Current Assets					
Cash and Equivalents	$ 560.0	$ 796.0	$ 44.4	$ 15.8	$ 24.9
Receivables	1,492.0	1,887.0	981.1	327.8	321.0
Inventories	622.0	676.0	447.9	322.8	328.1
Other Current Assets	1,226.0	1,228.0	521.4	110.6	174.4
Total Current Assets	$ 3,900.0	$ 4,587.0	$ 1,994.8	$ 776.5	$848.4
Non-Currents Assets					
Property, Plant & Equipment, Gross	31,799.0	40,627.0	25,286.7	23,726.1	23,307.9
Accumulated Depreciation & Depletion	8,159.0	17,760.0	6,715.7	6,127.6	5,562.2
Property, Plant & Equipment, Net	23,640.0	22,867.0	18,571.0	17,598.5	17,745.7
Intangibles	7,516.0	0.0	0.0	0.0	0.0
Other Non-Current Assets	5,685.0	12,060.0	4,308.2	3,000.7	2,941.7
Total Non-Current Assets	36,841.0	34,927.0	22,879.2	20,599.2	20,687.4
Total Assets	40,741.0	39,514.0	24,874.1	21,375.7	21,535.9
Liabilities & Shareholders Equity					
Current Liabilities					
Accounts Payables	1,442.0	1,747.0	879.6	336.4	300.7
Short-Term Debt	4,576.0	4,022.0	1,386.4	679.1	658.3
Other Current Liabilities	2,379.0	2,507.0	1,256.0	643.8	753.6
Total Current Liabilities	8,397.0	8,276.0	3,522.0	1,659.3	1,712.6
Non-Current Liabilities					
Long Term Debt	16,325.0	15,133.0	8,759.4	8,668.1	9,174.6
Deferred Income Taxes	3,938.0	3,718.0	2,989.3	2,801.6	2,669.8
Other Non-Current	2,197.0	2,737.0	1,560.5	1,129.6	1,112.8

Sample data for illustrative purposes only.

But, as you look at the liability side of the equation, it shows that current liabilities have gone up well out of proportion to the growth of the assets. In fact, Texas Utilities shows an increase in its overall liabilities by a greater percentage than the expansion of its assets. This caused the ratios to change, and the company seemed to be valued at the higher end of the spectrum by some, even in relation to its own history. The debt/equity ratio illustrates the increase very dramatically and the corresponding price/book suffers as the net assets are decreased.

In summary, many investors may have punished the company for utilizing high levels of debt. Of course, this does not take into account any macroeconomic conditions that may have played important roles in the actual movement of the sector or industry.

Another issue is the large increase in accounts receivable. This shows what monies are outstanding for goods or services already sold. Receivables have jumped dramatically on a year-to-year basis. If customers are slower to pay Texas Utilities, there may be rightful concern that the company might need to consider creating a higher allowance for bad debt. This means that the company will virtually give away services for free, which will undoubtedly cause earnings to decrease.

Inventories are another area to study. Utility companies will probably see very little increase on goods purchased, since customers utilize energy and affiliated services somewhat equally year to year. Of course, there are cold snaps, heat waves, and other heavy usage periods that will cause inventories to decrease. Even so, usage over time is relatively consistent.

Now, if a company is seen to have increasing inventories, it should sound the alarm that it may not be making the best use of planning and logistics. The world relies on 24/7, "just in time" product delivery, and companies had better "just in time" themselves to the 21st century. Large inventories could mean outdated product and distribution procedures, and therefore an allowance should be made for the real possibility of eventual inventory write-offs and write-downs. This could happen when inventories grow to the point where companies are agreeable to sell excess at a significant discount. This is in an effort to clear the warehouse shelves and recoup some of the costs associated with the manufacturing process.

Sample Ratios - Texas Utilities

	Price/ Book	Book Value per Share	Debt/Equity Ratio	Interest Coverage
Year 5	1.18	$30.15	1.96	2.0
Year 4	1.60	$29.21	1.84	2.0
Year 3	1.49	$27.90	1.28	2.4
Year 2	1.52	$26.86	1.44	2.4
Year 1	1.62	$25.38	1.60	0.7

Price Targets

Possibly the most overlooked aspect of fundamental analysis is the setting of appropriate price targets for both purchases and sales. As a disciplined investor, you can appreciate the importance of using guidelines in your investment plan to reduce risk. This will help your portfolio (and your emotions) fluctuate less.

Obviously, the first element in developing an appropriate price target is to gather information on the company in question. You need to understand what its forward-looking strategy is, as well as the overall economic environment in which it operates. Take as an example a company in the semiconductor industry.

It is a good idea for the owner of the company to under-stand the competition. Since you are planning on owning a piece of the company, here are a few sample questions you may want to think about:

- Who is the competition?
- Who are the suppliers, and who are the buyers?
- What effect do domestic and international economic events have on their products?
- Will a weakening currency cause a change in the demand for their products?
- Will they purchase supplies from international vendors that can be affected by the dollar or any other cross-currency exchange issues?
- Do their competitors have similar pricing structures?
- Is the product-set outdated?
- What costs are associated with new research and development?
- Is there any concentration risk?
- Are they reliant on one supplier or buyer?
- Is there a particular industry, region or country that is important to the company?
- If a competitor drops the price on a main product, does the action affect the companies in question?
- Will they continue to have earnings momentum similar to their historical periods?
- Is their inventory up to date?
- Is management geared to distribute at the levels necessary?

Most of these questions can only be answered through significant amounts of research. Fortunately, services such as Thompson First Call, Zacks, Standard & Poor's, and others through individual brokerage houses can do this for you.

Actually, employing a service is a great way for you to receive earnings estimates for a company. It helps to streamline the process and give quality estimates of forward earnings from professionals that are studying them daily. Of course you could purchase subscriptions directly from these companies, but the costs are quite prohibitive for the average investor. A better idea would be to register with either *MSN Money* or *Quicken.com*. Both of these sites provide adequate earnings data—for free.

Once you have these tools in hand, you can begin the forecasting process by combining the range of estimates given with the answers you have gathered to the questions about the company.

So, if you have a range of analysts' estimates for stocks such as Bank of America that fall between $0.30 and $0.42, you can use your understanding of the markets to choose the estimate you feel most comfortable with. If you are not confident choosing a number, use the *average* of all of the available analysts' predictions. Then a formula that includes the earnings and projected growth rate can be used with any spreadsheet program. The result will provide you with a 12-month price target to use for both the purchase and the eventual sale of a security.

Price Target Examples:

Stock ABC	
EPS $4.00 Current	
$4.50 Forward (1 Year)	
$6.00 Forward (2 Year)	
$7.50 Forward (3 Year)	
5-Year Earnings Growth Estimate = 15%	
Current P/E Ratio = 10	
PEG Ratio (5yr) = 0.66	

12-Month Price Target

(Current P/E X Expected Earnings = Target)

10 x $4.50 = $45.00

24-Month Price Target (Conservative)
Forward P/E X Expected Earnings = Price Target
1) Forward P/E=$40 (current price)/$4.50 (forward EPS)
2) Expected Earnings = EPS (+2 Years)
8.8 X $6.00 = $53.00
24-Month Price Target (Aggressive)
Current P/E X Expected Earnings = Price Target
10 X $6.00 = $60.00

This chapter has elaborated on the fact that researching a company is no easy task. With so many different constructs and metrics at the disposal of the average investor, it is not surprising that many people are fearful of making a severe mistake. With so much to analyze, there is much room for failure or misinterpretation.

Fortunately, for the cautious investor there is a solution. In the industry it is known as risk management, and it was born out of the market's sometimes-rocky past. With a nod to its application, however, any investor can rest comfortably knowing that his or her assets are just as safe as they want them to be.

Just as no two investment approaches are alike, no two risk management plans are identical. There are many innovative solutions to choose from. The chapter that follows outlines the most significant of the bunch.

Chapter 5

Risk Management

As we discussed in Chapter 1, understanding your risk tolerance is a big step toward obtaining financial security. Understanding the emotions that you may go through during market instability will allow you to set up appropriate "insurance policies," helping to save your portfolio from the devastating effects of a crash.

📖 RISK MANAGEMENT
Analysis of possible loss: the profession or technique of determining, minimizing, and preventing accidental loss. For example, this could be accomplished when a business takes specific safety measures or buys liability insurance.

The above may be a suitable definition for the financial professional, but what exactly *is* risk management and for the individual investor, how does it fit into the scheme of things?

The exact definition of a "market crash" is unclear. Is it more than a bear market? Is it a sudden or prolonged downward spiral? Is it a 10 percent, 15 percent, or 20 percent correction? Studying the phenomenon of market crashes will help to better explain the effects. As an example, let's look at what occurred in 1987.

The headline and story in the *Wall Street Journal* for October 20, 1987 read:

Stocks Plunge 508.32 Amid Panicky Selling
For Houston secretary Julie Ianotti, a hard-won retirement nest egg suddenly looked very much in peril. "I'm scared," she told a reporter. "Should I sell? Tell me, should I sell?"

There were a lot of people who felt that way on "Black Monday," as it is called. It sent a wave of dread through a nation intoxicated on its own prosperity. During Reagan's presidency the trickle-down effect supported a loose monetary policy that spawned an "easy money" culture. Between January of 1980 and late summer of 1987, stocks had skyrocketed more than 225 percent. When they plunged 30 percent in a matter of weeks—mostly on that hard-to-forget, 508-point day—the nation was dumbfounded and left wondering what went wrong.

Forbes magazine ran a similar piece:

Black Monday and Red Faces
OCT. 19, 1987 was a stomach-twisting day for Wall Street and the nation. In a single trading session the Dow Jones Industrials dropped 508 points, and $480 billion in market value was expunged. The euphoria of a five-year bull market was shattered.

That crash was a terrifying event for the American people, but with hindsight we know that it provided one of the greatest buying opportunities of all time. Had you purchased $10,000 worth of a simple S&P 500 stock index fund after the crash and reinvested the dividends, you would have almost $50,000 today. That is a compounded annual return of 17 percent!

However, that was not what people were thinking about in late October 1987. They were looking back, not forward. The question that was going through everyone's mind was: "Is it going to be Black Tuesday 1929 all over again?"

A market free-fall is about the scariest thing imaginable for anyone who has invested their faith and hard earned money into stocks. That emotion has more to do with fear of the unknown than actual financial damage.

Sure, if you put your money to work at the top of the market in 1987 and did nothing else, even through the crash, you would have recouped all of the losses as early as the summer of 1989. Yet most people do not just sit back and let the market do its work. Instead they prefer to dollar cost average money into the market from their paycheck into pension plans and other savings accounts. Moreover, they often attempt to time the market and usually end up being wrong.

Prior to 1987, you would have had to go back almost six decades—way back to 1929—to find a time when Wall Street was so vulnerable. The difference between the two corrections was primarily the depth and breadth of the occurrence. The infamous crash of 1929 lasted longer and had a far greater effect on the populace. In fact, many people were financially wiped out permanently and plenty of others never fully recovered mentally. On the other hand, the 1987 correction was short-lived and the recovery was rather quick.

Looking back at the events that led up to the 1929 crash, history shows the U.S. stock market had peaked on the first Tuesday of September 1929. The DJIA stood at a record of 381 and started a smooth, seemingly innocent downturn throughout the rest of the month. By the end of the September, the index was down 10 percent.

During the first 19 days of October, the index had lost another 8 percent and was now hovering at 15 percent below its recent peak.

Margin calls started to go out by brokerage houses and investors were very anxious. Then, on Monday, October 19, 1929, the heavy selling began. Within two days, the market dropped another six percent.

Over the next few days, the markets seemed to have settled down and there was talk that the worst was over. The daily volatility moderated and many investors were elated as they believed the correction had run its course. It was time to reassess, think about what had happened, and put some funds back into the market at these lower prices. What they didn't know was that they were smack in the middle of the eye of the storm. It was not over by any means.

Now remembered as Black Thursday, October 24 was the day when six New York banks needed to step in to intervene in an attempt to stabilize the markets. By day's end, the Wall Street roller coaster had seen enormous peaks and valleys. Amazingly though, the market closed *off* only 2 percent off for the day.

Nonetheless, the sell-off, with its many interruptions, continued. The 1929 low came on November 13 at a level of 199—almost half the value of the previous market's peak.

It was not until July 2, 1932 that the index reached a dramatic low of 41. In the end, more than three tortuous years had passed from the time the DJIA had reached its highest peak to when it dipped to its lowest valley—almost a 90 percent loss.

Most of the world's stock markets crashed right along with Wall Street in both 1929 and 1987. Once again the distinct difference was that the 1929 crash was much more sustained and deep. Also, the 1987 crash was shown to be quick and abrupt. In 1987, most investors recognized that it was a "contained" American catastrophe, not a world crisis.

Another differentiation is that after the 1929 crash there was a grave blunder by the government regarding monetary policy. Essentially, it zigged when it should have zagged. This is what eventually led to the Depression of the 1930s.

This is not to say that the 1987 crash was not without its governmental *faux pas*. That time, however, the mistake was made to the other extreme—creating a *loose* monetary policy. In time this mistake led to the explosive inflation that Americans experienced during the late 1980s.

While there are several definitions available for the term "Market Crash," let us agree that a market crash is represented by a substantial drop the in value of stocks and stock markets. The truth is that a stock market never goes up in a straight line, so there are bound to be crashes and/or corrections along the way. It can take a few days, months, or even years for a market to recover after a crash or correction.

For example, think back to March of 2000 to revisit the highest high of both the NASDAQ and DJIA. If only there could have been an insurance policy to stop the losses… If only we had seen it coming… If only we had gotten out sooner… If only we had…

Fortunately, there are steps that can be taken to help prevent your portfolio from being decimated by a market correction. By following risk management disciplines, the type of excruciating pain and mental anguish that most investors endured during 2000-2002 can be avoided. Now you have the tools enabling you to be much more consistent and ultimately more successful. In Chapter 9 you will earn how to organize your portfolio to allow differing asset classes to work harmoniously. The science of diversification will be introduced and explored as one type of risk management.

Intuitively, we all know that we should have some forms of insurance on our lives, our homes, and our automobiles. It is truly unfortunate that only a small percentage of individual investors have ever considered buying some type of insurance for their portfolios. The only possible explanation is that brokers and financial advisors do not believe that individuals have the capacity to understand these techniques—after all, they are more difficult concepts to learn than simply investing in a mutual fund. Yet given a little patience (along with user-friendly information) *you* can learn to understand them.

If the market crash discussions did not persuade you to give this topic serious thought, maybe some quick points will help to drive home how a portfolio should react and why portfolio insurance is so important. While you may actually be able to buy "portfolio insurance" through an annuity or possibly from specialized insurance companies, what you will learn here mainly deals with protection and risk reduction rather than an actual insurance policy.

Quite often, questions regarding portfolio volatility and performance expectations are on the minds of investors. Usually they want to know the risk of loss and the opportunity for gain. More importantly though, a *Disciplined Investor* is looking to take on the risk associated with upside gain yet wants to limit the potential for loss. The following analogy effectively explains this important concept.

Sit back and relax for a moment. Now, picture yourself walking down the street of a busy metropolis with buildings as tall as 100 floors. You enter a building and walk through the lobby and arrive at the elevators. The doors slowly open and you step inside. As you look at the panel of potential floor selections, you quickly notice that there are 100 buttons for the floors above you and four for the floors below.

This is exactly how a portfolio should operate on a long-term basis. It should have good upside potential while limiting the downside. The "skyscraper approach" to investing can be done quite effectively through disciplines of diversification, protective puts, covered calls, and a few other strategies that you will soon learn how to master.

Now, picture of a flower garden. To have a gorgeous garden with flowers in bloom throughout the year, you would not want to simply plant annuals. Sure, they would look gorgeous for the few months that they were in bloom, but they *would* eventually die. Only stems would remain as a depressing reminder of the beauty that once was.

Most gardens, like most portfolios, have far better plans in place. Perennials, annuals, and even evergreens create an assortment that will have something in bloom at any given time of the year. Even during the harsh winter, the evergreens remain fully colored and full of life.

Now, try to bridge these concepts as they relate to your portfolio. How many of us had cash positions (garden-speak: evergreens) during a significant market downturn? Did we overdo it a "bit" in the technology area (garden-speak: were we only planting impatiens and flowering plants)? What about those investors who had a large percentage of their holdings in only a few stocks that, at the time, they were completely head over heals, madly in love with (garden-speak: that big tree that Grandpa loved and would never trim which fell on the house when the big storm came)?

Any of these analogies can be all too real. You need to be aware of your personal influence(s) when constructing a solid, disciplined portfolio.

No worthy discussion of risk management would be complete without touching on the topic of **market timing**.📖 There are many different forms of market timing, but for our purposes, we will focus on simply buying in and selling out of equity markets.

These strategies represent attempts to either create profits or reduce losses. If you have the time, the desire, or both, try an Internet search for *market-timing strategies*. You will find that there are plenty of websites that will fill you in on all the details of, and provide you with incredible claims of fortunes made by, market timing programs.

While researching information for this book, websites were uncovered that claimed to have developed methods for making *thousands* of percents in profits on an annual basis. All it took for you to have the same experience was a paid subscription to their secret and "exclusive" market timing programs. Oddly, most of these claims ended in either 1999 or 2000. Not much more information was available, and it was painfully obvious that substantial upside results were not recorded during those periods anyway.

📖 MARKET TIMING
Trying to buy or sell investments and/or enter or exit the market at the right time by anticipating when prices are going to rise or fall.

The important word to focus on in the above definition is "*trying*." It describes the process of market timing rather well. In this definition, "trying" has a dual meaning. First, it refers to *trying* to find the optimal time to buy and/or sell a stock. Second, it refers to the realization of how *trying* an experience it is.

For years, investors have hoped that market timing would be the miraculous solution to the problem of limiting losses during periodic market corrections. Unfortunately, it rarely seems to work out that way. The *art* of market timing has never really been proven as a scientific strategy that could be adopted by the majority within the investment community—though there have been some revered prognosticators who were elevated to Investment Gods after certain very timely predictions.

Elaine Garzarelli, probably the best known market timer, accurately predicted the market crash of 1987. It has been reported that since then, she has called market tops, only to find that the markets were headed much higher.

With this fine example, what they say about the practice of market timing seems to be true: "Eventually, a market timer will be right, just the same as a broken clock is right two times every day." Be wary of predictions, substantial and overstated claims, and incredible fortunes made by market timers. Look closely and you will find that quite often they are merely offering you historical returns based on one particular stock or one particular mutual fund style.

Rather than an exhaustive diatribe on the disadvantages of *authentic* market timing, we will take a peek into how market timers have fared. To fairly illustrate the results of the predictors, we have gathered information from the pages of *SmartMoney* (a joint publishing venture from Dow Jones & Company, Inc. and Hearst Communications—see www.smartmoney.com).

SmartMoney has done a terrific job of researching and reviewing the predictions of high-profile market prognosticators. Some are economists, while others are analysts. *SmartMoney* acquires its pundits' predictions from two major sources: Dow Jones News Retrieval (which gives them stories from all major business publications, newspapers, and newswires) and all of the market-strategy reports that their experts send directly to their clients (for example, David Jones's "Monthly Market Commentary" or Ed Hyman's "Money and Markets Summary").

After receiving the Dow Jones News Retrieval predictions electronically, the researchers at *SmartMoney* disregard, "pithy quotes from pundits who comment on yesterday's markets and therefore do not discuss the markets' future." Then, at the end of each month, they keep only the cleanest predictions—clear and decisive calls about one of the several important market indicators such as:

- The DJIA and S&P 500 Index
- The Fed
- Interest Rates
- The Economy
- The 30-Year Treasury Bond Yield
- Individual Stocks or Sectors

Their research only dates back to January 1, 1995, yet the markets have thrown many curves along the way to help trip up the experts. Therefore, the outcome could be considered a good showing of their accuracy.

Smart Money's "Pundit Scorecard"	
Pundit/Analyst	Score/Rating
Abby Joseph Cohen	66.20%
Edward Kerschner	62.50%
Byron Wien	58.70%
David Jones	56.50%
Edward Hyman	56.50%
Ralph Acampora	55.90%
Elaine Garzarelli	55.70%
Edward Yardeni	54.80%
Barton Biggs	50.90%
Jeff Applegate	48.90%
Joe Battipaglia	48.50%
Thomas Galvin	47.00%

*Ending June, 2001   Historical Example
                                  (Source: Smart Money)

To calculate their pundits' batting averages, they take the predictions made by each of them since the beginning date and then figure in each successive call. Then they see if it was accurate or not. For example, in June 2001 they used all the pundits' calls from January 1, 1995 through May 31, 2001.

Are you surprised to learn that the group was generally less than average at predicting the markets? These are the people making headlines daily. Despite that fact, it seems pretty obvious that good and enduring investment disciplines should not be built around types of individual predictions—as on average they only have a 50/50 possibility of being correct.

One final point on market timing, and then we will move on. There are four possible outcomes for a market prediction. If the prediction is correct, you win…right? Well, maybe. Take a look at the table below to find out more about the possible outcomes of predictions made by market timers.

Action	If Prediction Is Correct	If Prediction Is Incorrect
	-You Will Receive-	
Buy Stocks	Market Performance	Significant Loss
Sell Stocks	Money Market Returns	Money Market Returns

Only two of the four possibilities will yield market returns. Explained another way, you have a 50 percent chance of participating in the growth or loss of the market with a *good* market timer. If you add that to the 50 percent batting average that the "cream of the crop" scored, you are now down to a 25 percent probability of positive participation in the market. Those are not the odds that you should want for your portfolio.

At this point, you are undoubtedly stuffed with information about the advantages and/or disadvantages of market timing. Hopefully, you agree that removing this strategy from the list of risk management ideas to help manage risk within a portfolio is wise. So, with that gone, what is left? Only the *two* best ways to keep your profits: covered call options and protective puts.

Each of these methods can be used in such ways as to allow you to keep maximum gains while at the same time reducing losses. Does that sound like the Holy Grail of investing?

Let us start by outlining the background of (and introduction to) a topic known simply as "options." According to their own published history, the Chicago Board Options Exchange (CBOE) was founded in 1973. It is an initiative that systematically revolutionized options trading by creating standardized, listed stock options. Prior to the year of its foundation, options were traded on an unregulated basis and were not required to adhere to the principle of "fair and orderly markets."

Investors quickly accepted these new options, propelling the CBOE to the status of second-largest securities exchange in the country and the world's largest options exchange. Today, CBOE accounts for more than half of all U.S. options trading and an amazing 91 percent of all index options trading.

Even though the CBOE was originally created by the Chicago Board of Trade (CBOT), it has always been managed and regulated as an independent entity. This is important to note because it means that there are layers of checks and balances in place to provide for oversight.

On April 26, 1973, after four years of solid planning, the doors of the CBOE were finally opened for business. In the beginning, it was limited to trading call options on only 16 underlying stocks. It was not until 1977, however, that put options were introduced. Only two years thereafter additional securities exchanges began entering the business. Today, options are traded on four U.S. exchanges, including the CBOE. Even with these additions, the CBOE is still considered the busiest options exchange in the world.

History out of the way, you are about to learn all you ever may want to know about the investment known as "options."

Simply put, an option is a contract giving the buyer the right, but not the obligation, to buy or sell an underlying asset (a stock or index) at a specific price on or before a certain date. Listed options are contracts for 100 shares of the particular underlying asset.

Options are securities, similar to bonds and stocks. The difference is that they are not actually ownership in the company. Rather, they are a contract to buy or sell the underlying shares of a company.

Options contracts contain very strict provisions and have many fine details that need to be reviewed before an investment is made. Even though there are essentially only two types of options (calls and puts) there are several dozen different investment techniques used by options investors. Some only include the use of a call or put, while more complicated strategies may involve several puts, calls, or even shares of an underlying stock. The bread and butter of these is the covered call strategy.

📖 COVERED CALLS

A covered call is the process of both owning a stock and selling a call option against that stock. It can also be the purchase of a stock and the synchronized sale of a call against that stock purchase. For the most part, these transactions are often paired in 100 share lots.

By "writing" or "selling" the call, the investor receives a premium and in return will be obligated to sell the stock to the buyer at a predetermined price. Said another way, the

investor/writer is paid money in return for a contract to sell the
stock to another party at a predetermined price for a specific
period of time. The writer of the covered call, in return for the
premium paid, will essentially give up his rights to the profit of
the stock above a certain price, also known as the strike price.

The use of **covered calls**📖 works well in most types of
portfolios, but it may not be permitted in some accounts such
as IRA's and certain pension plans. While this is a risk reduction strategy and is available to most investors, it may not be
suitable for all. Since there is a much greater degree of experience required, care should be taken to understand the basic
components of options before entering into any transaction.

Who should consider covered call options?

- An investor who is desirous of protecting the risk
  associated with the downside losses in his portfolio.
- An investor who is looking to trade some upside
  opportunity for risk reduction.
- An investor who would like to receive income
  payments in addition to the regular dividends paid
  from a stock he or she is holding.

One of the benefits of the covered call strategy is that the
premium📖 received can be calculated into the cost structure
of a stock purchase, effectively reducing the price paid. Also,
the holder of the stock will collect dividends from his or her
holding (if any) until the position is sold. Even so, while the
investor has reduced the cost and thereby helped to reduce
risk, if the price of the stock surpasses the strike price of the
option the investor will not participate in any additional gains.

📖   PREMIUM

The amount that a buyer needs to pay for a call or put option. This grants them the right to buy or sell a stock or index at a predetermined price at some time in the future.

Currently, stock ZYX is priced at $41.75 and the investor thinks that this might be a good purchase. Three-month 45 calls can be sold for $1.25. Historically, ZYX has paid a quarterly dividend of $0.25. By selling the three-month 45 call, the investor is agreeing to sell ZYX at $45 should the owner of the call decide to **exercise**📖 his or her right to buy the stock.

📖   EXERCISE (OPTION)

The act of implementing the right to either buy or sell a security (as with a call option). Exercising an option is basically another term for taking action on an owned security.

Remember that the owner of the call option has the right to exercise the option at any time. Until it reaches $45 that would not make much financial sense. Once it moves past the strike price, the owner will be able to buy the stock at a price lower than it is currently trading in the open markets.

Take a look at what happens to a covered call position as the underlying stock moves up or down. Commissions have not been taken into consideration in these examples; however, they *can* have a significant impact on returns.

Transaction: *1) Buying 100 ZYX at $41.75 and*
2) Selling 1 Three-Month 45 Call at $1.25

Below are three possible scenarios provided by the CBOE. Note that all discussions assume option expiration.

Scenario 1: ZYX remains below $45 between now and expiration—call not assigned.
The call option will expire, worthless. The premium of $1.25 and the stock position will be retained. In effect, you have paid $40.50 (which is also the breakeven price) for ZYX ($41.75 purchase cost minus $1.25 premium received for sale of the call). This would be offset by any dividends that were received, which, in this example, were $0.25.

When the ZYX call expires worthless, the covered call writer can sell another call going further out in time, taking in additional premiums. Once again, this produces an even lower purchase cost or breakeven point.

If ZYX remains below $45 for an entire year, the investor can sell these calls four times. For this example, we will make the hypothetical assumption that the price of the stock and option premiums remain constant throughout the year.
$1.25 (Call Premium Received) x 4 = $5 in Premium;
Premiums Received + Dividends Received = Total Income

Scenario 2: ZYX rises above $45 between now and expiration—call assigned.
The call buyer can exercise his right to buy the stock, and the call seller will have to sell ZYX at $45, even though ZYX has risen above $45. But remember, the call seller has taken in the premium of the call and has been earning dividends (if any) on the stock.

If ZYX stock is called away at expiration:

1) Receive	$ 45.00 per share (from stock sale/exercise)	$ 4,500.00
2) Add	$ 1.25 per share (premium)	$ 125.00
	(Total Proceeds from Strategy)	$ 4,625.00
3) Subtract	$ 41.75 (cost per share)	$ 4,175.00
	GAIN*	$ 450.00

* In three months, plus dividends (if any) received.

Scenario 3: ZYX is right at $45 at expiration.

At expiration, the seller of a call may be in a scenario similar to either one or two as discussed above. There is also the chance that the stock is right at the strike price when it expires. The option buyer may require the stock to be called away, and the call writer will be obligated to sell ZYX at $45.

Alternatively, the stock may not be called away and the option will expire worthless. The writer can then use the strategy of selling another call, going further out in time, bringing in additional premium, and further reducing the breakeven point.

Covered Calls Summary

When an investor writes a covered call, it meets a good deal of investment needs by helping to reduce risk while still keeping some of the upside opportunity in play. The actual strategy can be used in many different types of accounts for a defensive position on a stock that the investor is considering, or one that the investor currently owns. Amazingly, there are more than 1,700 listed options for stocks and more that 200 that are considered LEAPS® (Long-term Equity AnticiPation Securities).

LEAPS® are for a longer term than the standard equity related options and are often linked to stock indices'. There are also numerous choices of options types available today and a very active market for investors to trade. This is primarily due to the fact that options as an investment choice have come back into "vogue."

The strategy of utilizing covered calls is actually considered less aggressive than just owning the stock on its own. Since premiums are received in return for the obligation to sell at a specific price at a later date, the breakeven point for the position has been lowered, thus allowing for a greater margin of error in the buy discipline.

Protective Puts as a Hedge

Think of purchasing a protective put against stock as you might think of purchasing insurance: the premium is paid in order to insure against the potential loss inherent in stock ownership. Regardless of which direction the stock's price moves, the holder of the protective put can automatically sell as soon as it reaches the strike price.

First, before getting into the specifics of protective puts, consider who should think about investing in them.

- If you already hold a stock that you think may rise in value, but you do not wish to take part in the risk of a fall, you may be interested in protecting your interests with a put.
- If you are considering purchasing a stock but are concerned that it could take a dive, a protective put may be right for you.

The stock market remains a volatile investment avenue. During bullish periods, investors often find themselves anxious about market corrections. During bear markets, they typically are worried about continuing declines.

The first reaction of most people is to avoid the situation altogether. But, considering the extraordinary potential for profit in the markets, this is not always the most appropriate course of action. Missing a strong upward move in the market would be an unfortunate circumstance.

Fortunately, puts protect against any reluctance you may have toward investing. It is strange to think that for centuries people did not blink an eye when it came to the concept of insuring a tangible asset, but it has taken so long for the strategy of insuring a commodity such as a stock position to become popular.

A protective put requires the purchase of what is known as a put contract. Each put contract covers 100 shares of stock that the investor is either buying or already owns. This put contract grants the owner the right to sell the covered security at a pre-established price. There is never any obligation involved in a protective put.

The contracts can be made to carry expiration dates of up to eight months in the future. As many as 1,700 stocks may be covered under this strategy. For a contract that stretches out as far as three years, only 200 stocks may be protected. The latter category is referred to as LEAPS®, which was mentioned earlier.

Knowing what protective puts are allows you to examine the effects they have on an otherwise unpredictable stock position. Take note: these examples do not take commissions into consideration.

How to Use a Protective Put
Now we will discuss the three possible scenarios at the expiration of a put contract as provided by the CBOE.

Scenario 1: Buy ZYX at $50.
First, let us look at buying a stock without owning a put for protection. If stock is bought at $50 per share, as soon as it drops below the purchase price the investor begins to lose money. The entire $50 purchase price is at risk. Of course, if the price increases, the investor benefits from the entire increase without incurring the cost of the put premium or insurance.

When you buy a stock, there is no protection or insurance. Therefore, you are at risk of losing the total investment.

Scenario 2: Buy ZYX at $50, Buy ZYX 50 Put.
Let us look at a scenario in which ZYX is bought with a protective put. In this example, ZYX is still at $50 per share. A 6-month put with a strike price of $50 can be bought for $2.25 or $225 per contract ($2.25 x $100).

This scenario of utilizing a put "at-the-money" can be thought of as insurance without a deductible. Since the stock is bought at $50 and the put has the same strike price, a drop in the share price of the stock will have little effect on the net portfolio value for the investor. This allows for an investor to effectively reduce the risk on a stock or a portfolio during volatile market conditions.

	Buy ZYX Only		Buy ZYX and 6-month *50 put option*	
Stock Cost	$	50.00	$	50.00
Put Cost	$	-	$	2.25
Total Cost	$	50.00	$	52.25
Risk	$	50.00	$	2.25

Even if the price of ZYX falls, the investor that bought the six-month put option with a strike price of $50 has the right to sell it at $50 through the expiration date. The savvy option investor has limited the risk of that position to only $2.25, which is the premium paid for the put.

Since a "near-the-money" put was purchased, this investment strategy provides benefits of limited downside protection and does not limit the upside as we have seen with other option approaches. The limitation is that the investor will need to see the stock rise above $52.25 in order to achieve a profit from this trade. If the stock maintains its price without moving up, the put will eventually expire with no value and the premium will vanish.

In contrast, if the stock were bought without an option strategy, the investor would profit as soon as the stock price moved beyond $50. Yet there would not be protection afforded against the risk of the stock's price falling. By utilizing a put option along with a stock purchase, the investor benefits. Risk is reduced and the potential for gain is maintained.

Scenario 3: Buy ZYX at $50, Buy ZYX 45 Put.
Perhaps an investor would rather have some downside protection with a small deductible. This strategy will reduce the cost

of portfolio insurance by purchasing an "out-of-the-money" put option along with the stock purchase.

If the put has a $45 strike price and the underlying stock is at $50, it can be said that you have effectively purchased insurance with a $5 deductible (per share). The put will provide a counterbalance if the stock moves below $45 per share. At that point the investor can make the choice of exercising the put—thereby selling the stock or selling the put. The basis for the decision will depend on where the investor believes the bottom will be. If he or she believes the stock is at its base, they will probably sell the put.

If the stock is under $45, the put will be valued at least somewhere between where the stock price is trading in the open markets and the strike price of the put option. The profit from the sale of the put can be used to offset the losses from the stock's position. If there is no more hope for the stock, the stock can be sold. If, on the other hand, the stock has the opportunity to move up again, the profits from the put can be realized and the stock's rise will further enhance the investor's portfolio performance.

The problem with this strategy is the investor will have to see a rise in the stock above $51 before a profit is realized since in the example there is a $1-per-share cost to buy the option. If the investor did not use the option plan and only bought the stock at $50, he would begin to profit from the investment above his share cost. However, the lack of a defensive position will leave the investor open to the risk of losing the full value of the initial purchase.

	Buy ZYX No Options	Buy ZYX and buy 6-month *50 put*	Buy ZYX and buy 6-month *45 put*
Stock Cost	$ 50.00	$ 50.00	$ 50.00
Put Cost	$ -	$ 2.25	$ 1.00
Total Cost	$ 50.00	$ 52.25	$ 51.00
Risk	$ 50.00	$ 2.25	$ 6.00

Applying the correct strategies when buying an "at-the-money" or an "out-of–the-money" put helps to reduce risk in a portfolio. At the same time, each has advantages and disadvantages. Either way, the intent is to provide a touch of portfolio insurance while maintaining a degree of upside potential.

Protective Puts Give You Options

In the past, options have been given a bad name. Maybe it was because of the lack of understanding or possibly the known abuses within the industry. Today, with a new sense of what certain options can do for a portfolio, the benefits can be better recognized. The choices available are many when using puts as a protective mechanism within a portfolio. For example, a put with a strike price of $55 might cost $1.25 per share or $125 per contract. This 55 put gives the investor the right to sell ZYX at $55. With this position, he can continue to hold the stock, hoping it will rise further while knowing that he can always sell it for a profit of $3.75 (sell at the $55 strike price minus the $50 stock purchase price minus the $1.25 put cost) no matter how far the stock falls.

When investors are buying the same type of puts over and over, it is considered "rolling." This will provide a good deal of flexibility so that the investor can adjust the strike price as the price of the underlying stock moves, but it will also create higher costs due to commissions. This needs to be considered carefully to ensure that there can be profitable transactions, net of fees.

Protective Puts Summary

Investors are always looking to find ways to reduce risk in a portfolio. As investors are inherently "risk adverse," the purchase of a protective put is a good way to supply an ample amount of relief from the fear of losing money.

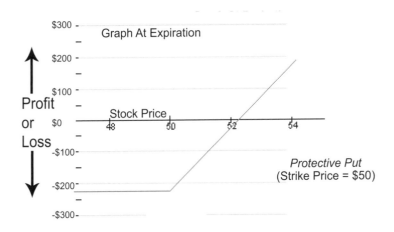

By now, you will hopefully agree that the use of a protective put and other options strategies will actually create a layer of support and protection which can help to reduce risk within a portfolio. While the advantages clearly outweigh the disadvantages, there is an important fact you need to remember: profits can only be realized after the costs of the options purchase are subtracted and the stock moves past a certain calculated level. Additionally, the put option has a finite lifespan. This last point will require accurate tracking to ensure that once the option expires, another protective put strategy will be implemented.

Several key protective strategies have been outlined in this chapter. While it is good to consider each of these risk management factors, the critical point to remember is that no portfolio—regardless of its level of protection—is completely safe from all potential risks, even if it is properly diversified. As a result of this fundamental concept, the idea of the mutual fund was conceived.

While the mutual fund can be viewed as a form of investment strategy with diversification built right in, it is not in itself a complete portfolio. You cannot simply dump all of your investable assets into one mutual fund and call it a day.

This is not to say that this tool does not have value, however. In fact, quite the contrary. Mutual funds are the core component of any balanced portfolio and disciplined investment strategy. In the next chapter you will learn why.

Chapter 6

Why Mutual Funds?

Mutual funds help to create a well-diversified portfolio. Using them not only helps you broaden your investment base, but it also provides you with assistance when researching investment sectors that are difficult to understand. They are also beneficial because:

- There are only so many hours in a day you can commit to research.
- The disciplines for mutual fund investing are not the same as those for stocks. The truth is funds need to be researched with an entirely different skill set.
- There are potential language barriers when investing internationally.
- Currency conversion/hedging may be difficult to implement for an individual investor.
- Information and research within certain sectors may be difficult to access.

Fortunately, this is a solution readily available to help investors find suitable investments in countries, sectors, and industries that they may not be able to research. This will allow you to focus your research within the areas you are strongest, and at the same time confidently handing off the remaining portfolio management responsibilities to a qualified fund manager.

The process of finding the best fund choice can be daunting as there are over 10,000 funds available today. Right now, there are more sectors covered than ever before. Looking forward, it seems likely that more specialty funds will be created rather than those that will simply invest according to an index. This is primarily due to the public's desire to have some control and involvement over its investments.

Looking back, mutual funds have a history dating back as far as the 19th century. At that time, labor groups and trade guilds within Europe often used the pooling of monies to purchase investments. Yet it was not until 1924 that the first true open-ended mutual fund was established. That fund, the Massachusetts Investors Trust, was the brainchild of Edward G. Leffler. Within the first year of operation, it successfully amassed over $392,000 from 200 excited investors.

Prior to the crash of 1929, there had been less than adequate financial disclosure; a **prospectus** had yet to be required. At that time, there existed only 21 funds with just $134 million of invested assets. In 1933, a sweeping change jolted the industry as congress adopted the *Securities Act of 1933*, requiring full disclosure by prospectus.

📖　PROSPECTUS

A prospectus is a formal notice filed with the SEC that outlines a company's intent to sell securities. This notice is required to contain every bit of information that might be valuable for an investor attempting to make an informed decision about whether to buy or sell a stock in that company.

At that time, funds did not gain much popularity, as they were a mystery to most. The fund industry's growth was also hampered by the fact that investing in the stock market did not come back into fashion again until the 1950s. Up until then, most investors still suffered a bad hangover from the great crash of the 1930s and were terrified of stocks. Bonds were therefore safer bets, since they were easily understood, and ultimately became the investment of choice for the average Jane and Joe.

Fast forward to the 1950s and the days of sock-hops and hot-rods. This period eventually gave birth to over 100 new funds for investors. This popularity continued to intensify as time passed into the 1960s. New funds came on strong and investors started to invest money at record rates. Unfortunately, just as soon as funds were becoming a popular investment vehicle, the stock market went through one of the worst corrections in over two decades.

From 1971 to 1973, the Dow Jones lost an average of 16.1 percent per year. With their investors furious, money flew out of equity funds and into the safety of CDs. It was not until the latter part of the 1970s and into the 1980s that the "me first" attitude was back in full swing again. This sounded the charge to investors wanting to catch the "profit wave." At the time, stocks were difficult to research and commission rates were outrageous. (During the early 1980s, buying 100 shares of a stock could have cost you $150 in fees alone.)

As such, the most obvious choice was to either give your broker full discretion (*not* a good idea) or buy a mutual fund.

Mutual fund sales soared again, further enhanced because of the fact that they paid a whopping commission to the selling broker. Fund companies saw their assets increase geometrically.

Jump forward to the latter part of the 90s, when there were more funds than anyone knew what to do with. Today, over 80 million Americans own mutual funds, with assets totaling more than $6 trillion. Investment styles range from value to growth, quantitative to fundamental, market correlated to neutral, and everything in between.

Even so, there are still some problems inherent to mutual fund investing, like window dressing and high fees. The good news is that if you carefully follow a regimented discipline to uncover the true strategy of the fund and research a few key statistics, you can probably avoid these pitfalls.

Mutual Funds Defined

A mutual fund is an investment company that allows shareholders to pool money with the intent to invest in a diversified portfolio of securities. Funds usually accept a minimum initial deposit of $250 or sometimes less by creating a systematic investment plan for only $25 per month. The benefit to investors is professional management and diversification. Whether investing $1,000 or $1,000,000, the investor will have an exact proportional percentage of the total fund holdings within their portfolio.

Suppose that Jeff and Sarah invest $10,000 into the Superior Stock Mutual Fund. Their respective holdings will be:

Percent Of Fund	Holding	Jeff and Sarah's Percentage
10%	Microsoft	10%
15%	Pfizer	15%
20%	General Electric	20%
25%	FNMA	25%
15%	Oracle	15%
15%	General Motors	15%

This is the case for all investors in this fund, since it is an open-end mutual fund. This means that as more money is deposited, additional fund shares are created. On the reverse side, as money is withdrawn, fund shares are redeemed. The end product amounts to unlimited shares with total liquidity. Ultimately, the process dictates daily pricing of the fund at 4:00 p.m. and more importantly, equality for all fund investors.

Fund Types

As previously mentioned, funds come in all shapes, sizes, and flavors. In order to get even more acquainted, a good starting point would be to break down the fund universe into four basic groups: Money Market Funds, Hybrid Funds, Equity Funds, and Bond Funds.

Total Net Assets of Mutual Funds *(billions of dollars)*

	Sept 06	Aug 06	% chg	Dec 05
Equity/Stock Funds	$5,455.5	$5,361.5	1.8	$4,939.8
Hybrid Funds	613.0	602.8	1.7	567.3
Taxable Bond Funds	1,086.4	1,077.2	0.9	1,018.5
Municipal Bond Funds	357.0	353.7	0.9	338.8
Taxable Money Market Funds	1,861.2	1,837.7	1.3	1,706.5
Tax-Free Money Market Funds	349.1	351.8	-0.8	334.0
Total	$9,722.2	$9,584.7	1.4	$8,904.8

(Source: Investment Company Institute)

From here, you can further define subcategories to help discover the appropriate fund for your portfolio.

Now that you know what broad categories are available, it is important to understand the more specific fund classifications. This will be especially useful when you start the screening process outlined later in this chapter.

According to the *Investment Company Institute*, funds can be further divided into many unique objective categories. Below are the common definitions.

MUTUAL FUND INVESTMENT OBJECTIVES

EQUITY FUNDS
Equity Funds primarily invest in common stocks with the objective of capital appreciation.

- **Capital Appreciation Funds,** as their name would suggest, seek capital appreciation; dividends are not a primary consideration.

- **Aggressive Growth Funds** invest primarily in common stocks of small growth companies.

- **Growth Funds** invest primarily in common stocks of well-established companies.

- **Sector Funds** invest primarily in companies within related fields.

- **Total Return Funds** seek a combination of current income and capital appreciation.

- **Growth-And-Income Funds** invest primarily in common stocks of established companies with the potential for growth and a consistent record of dividend payments.

- **Equity/Income Funds** invest primarily in equity securities of companies with consistent records of dividend payments. They seek income more than capital appreciation.

- **World Equity Funds** invest primarily in stocks of foreign companies.

- **Emerging Market Funds** invest primarily in companies based in developing regions of the world.

- **Global Equity Funds** invest primarily in equity securities traded worldwide, including those of U.S. companies.

- **International Equity Funds** must invest in equity securities of companies located outside the United States and cannot invest in U.S. company stocks.

- **Regional Equity Funds** invest in companies based in a specific part of the world.

HYBRID FUNDS

Hybrid Funds may invest in a mix of equities, fixed-income securities, and derivative instruments.

- **Asset Allocation Funds** invest in various asset classes including, but not limited to, equities, fixed-income securities, and money market instruments. They seek high total return by maintaining precise weightings in asset classes.

- **Global Asset Allocation Funds** invest in a mix of equity and debt securities issued worldwide.

- **Balanced Funds** invest in a mix of equity securities and bonds with the three-part objective of conserving principal, providing income, and achieving long-term growth of both principal and income. These funds maintain target percentages in asset classes.

- **Flexible Portfolio Funds** invest in common stocks, bonds, debt securities, and money market securities to provide high total return. These funds may invest up to 100 percent in any one type of security.

- **Income-Mixed Funds** invest in a variety of income-producing securities, including equities and fixed-income instruments. These funds seek a high level of current income without regard to capital appreciation.

TAXABLE BOND FUNDS

These are corporate bond funds that seek current income by investing in high-quality debt securities issued by U.S. corporations.

- **Corporate Bond Funds (General)** invest two-thirds or more of their portfolios in U.S. corporate bonds with no explicit restrictions on average maturity.

- **Corporate Bond Funds (Intermediate-Term)** invest two-thirds or more of their portfolios in U.S. corporate bonds with an average maturity of 5 to 10 years. These funds seek a high level of income with less price volatility than longer-term bond funds.

- **Corporate Bond Funds (Short-Term)** invest two-thirds or more of their portfolios in U.S. corporate bonds with an average maturity of one to five years. These funds seek a high level of income with less price volatility than intermediate-term bond funds.

- **High-Yield Bond Funds** invest two-thirds or more of their portfolios in lower-rated U.S. corporate bonds (BAA or lower by Moody's and BBB or lower by Standard and Poor's rating services).

- **World Bond Funds** invest in debt securities offered by foreign companies and governments. They seek the highest level of current income available worldwide.

- **Global Bond Funds (General)** invest in worldwide debt securities with no stated average maturity or an average maturity of five years or more. These funds may invest up to 25 percent of assets in companies located in the United States.

- **Global Bond Funds (Short-Term)** invest in debt securities worldwide with an average maturity of one to five years. These funds may invest up to 25 percent of assets in companies located in the United States.

- **Other World Bond Funds**, such as international bond and emerging market debt funds, invest in foreign government and corporate debt instruments. Two-thirds of an international bond fund's portfolio must be invested outside the United States.

- **Emerging Market Debt Funds** invest primarily in debt from underdeveloped regions of the world.

- **Government Bond Funds** invest in U.S. government bonds of varying maturities. They seek high current income.

- **Government Bond Funds (General)** invest two-thirds or more of their portfolios in U.S. government securities of no stated average maturity. Securities utilized by investment managers may change with market conditions.

- **Government Bond Funds (Intermediate-Term)** invest two-thirds or more of their portfolios in U.S. government securities with an average maturity of five to ten years. Securities utilized by investment managers may change with market conditions.

- **Government Bond Funds (Short-Term)** invest two-thirds or more of their portfolios in U.S. government securities with an average maturity of one to five years. Securities utilized by investment managers may change with market conditions.

- **Mortgage-Backed Funds** invest two-thirds or more of their portfolios in pooled mortgage-backed securities.

- **Strategic Income Funds** invest in a combination of U.S. fixed-income securities to provide a high level of current income.

TAX-FREE BOND FUNDS

State municipal bond funds invest primarily in municipal bonds issued by a particular state. These funds seek high after-tax income for residents within their individual states.

- **State Municipal Bond Funds (General)** invest primarily in single-state municipal bonds with an average maturity of greater than five years or no specific stated maturity. The income from these funds is largely exempt from federal as well as state income tax for residents of the state.

- **State Municipal Bond Funds (Short-Term)** invest primarily in single-state municipal bonds with an average maturity of one to five years. The income of these funds is largely exempt from federal as well as state income tax for residents of the state.

- **National Municipal Bond Funds** invest primarily in the bonds of various municipal issuers in the United States. These funds seek high current income free from federal tax.

- **National Municipal Bond Funds (General)** invest primarily in municipal bonds with an average maturity of more than five years or no specific stated maturity.

- **National Municipal Bond Funds (Short-Term)** invest primarily in municipal bonds with an average maturity of one to five years.

MONEY MARKET FUNDS

Taxable money market funds invest in short-term, high-grade money market securities and must have average maturities of 90 days or less. These funds seek the highest level of income consistent with preservation of capital. Maintaining a stable share price is a primary objective

- **Taxable Money Market Funds (Government)** invest primarily in U.S. Treasury obligations and other financial instruments issued or guaranteed by the U.S. government, its agencies, or its instrumentalities.

- **Taxable Money Market Funds (Non-Government)** invest primarily in a variety of money market instruments, including certificates of deposit from large banks, commercial paper, and bankers acceptances.

- **Tax-Exempt Money Market Funds** invest in short-term municipal securities and must have average maturities of 90 days or less. These funds seek the highest level of income free from federal (and, in some cases, state and local) taxes, consistent with preservation of capital.

- **National Tax-Exempt Money Market Funds** invest in short-term securities from various U.S. municipal issuers.

- **State Tax-Exempt Money Market Funds** invest primarily in short-term securities of municipal issuers in a single state to achieve the highest level of tax-free income for residents of that state.

Now that you are an "expert" on what types of mutual funds are available, the next thing you need to decide on is what you want a fund to do for you.

Take as an example John and Debbie. After spending some time assessing their risk tolerance and investment goals, they have designed an asset allocation that shows the need for a 10 percent position in high-yield bonds. Realizing that they have little experience in this area, they want to find a good mutual fund to help manage this portion of their plan.

Initially, they utilized Morningstar, the "source" for mutual fund information. They found it online and obtained a three-month trial subscription. They are now thinking about subscribing to the hard copy version to see what it may have that is different from the online version. Debbie also discovered a great deal of information about mutual funds at the *MSN Money* website—www.moneycentral.com. To her delight, everything there was available at no cost, so they decided to use both services until they have a better feel for what may be most appropriate for them.

To the surprise of John and Debbie, they find that there are 279 funds that are characterized as high-yield. What should they do now? They could easily look at the past performance and find the hottest funds over the past few years. Yet when they do this, they quickly realize that the underlying investments vary greatly. Some of the top-performing funds have bonds that are of questionable quality.

What John and Debbie need to do is use a discipline to uncover higher-costing underperformers. This can save a lot of aggravation and financial pain. For a number of years, some advisory firms have been working at refining their filtering and scoring systems. A good example of this is a system that aids in the search for funds to meet investment objectives that are included in portfolio allocations.

Here is some great news: You are about to gain access to a finely honed process that seeks out funds that both historically and presently have:

- Below average costs
- Limited style drift
- Low capital gain/dividend exposure
- Low risk factors
- High management tenure
- Consistency of returns/limited losses
- Statistically relevant characteristics

This may seem like an overwhelming list at first, but looking at each item one at a time may help.

Cost Factors

It may seem obvious to you, but it bears mentioning anyway: remember that the more it costs you to hold or invest in a fund, the lower your potential return. So if there are two index funds investing in the same sector, the one with the lower costs should have better long-term performance.

The 0.10 percent higher fee that Fund B charges comes directly out of your pocket. With this in mind, it is essential to find funds with below-average fees.

	Annual Expense Factor	5-Year Annualized Return	10-Year Annualized Return
Index Fund "A"	1.00%	15.00%	12.25%
Index Fund "B"	1.10%	14.42%	11.05%

To help you with some of the research, here are guidelines by fund sector/style:

<u>**Maximum Total Fee**</u>

Domestic Large Capitalization Funds	1.20%
Domestic Mid Capitalization Funds	1.30%
Domestic Small Capitalization Funds	1.35%
High-Yield Bond Funds	1.10%
International Stock Funds	1.50%
International Bond Funds	1.00%
Domestic Bond Funds	0.75%
Sector Funds	less than 2.00%

For the most part, newer funds will have higher expense ratios because they have fewer assets to spread their costs over. Sometimes the management and board of directors will decide to temporarily subsidize the annual costs until the fund has reached a size that will support these fees.

Watch out, though. You may be in for a hidden surprise a few years down the road when your annual expense ratio goes from 1.00 percent to 1.90 percent. Adding insult to injury is the fact that the only way you will find out is by conducting thorough research—the fund will *not* send you a friendly announcement about the rate change.

This is precisely why you want to stay away from new equity funds. New bond funds are even more problematic. When you invest in these, you have no idea what the ultimate portfolio will look like. Usually, the prospectus will allow for a wide range of investments available to the manager. You never know what you may get by blindly investing this way. Stick with bond funds that have fully invested portfolios with at least three years of historical performance statistics available.

Style Drift
This is a big no-no. Style drift, or changing the investment characteristics in the fund, is hard to pin down but it can be very destructive to your well-thought-out allocation.

This is the reason that index funds have gained such explosive popularity. An index fund is an investment vehicle that is designed to produce investment returns similar or identical to a specified index. These can be the DJIA, the Standard & Poor's 500, the Russell 3000, or any combination of these imaginable.

The fund manager accomplishes this either by replicating stocks held within the index in the same proportions or by buying other securities, such as futures and options contracts. The former is a much safer way to invest, however, since you hold stocks within the fund's portfolio rather than difficult to understand **derivatives**.

📖 DERIVATIVES

The word derivative has been used loosely to describe any investment that has been derived from another. An example is an option, which is a derivative of a stock. So, we can further refine the definition to state; "an investment which has its price based on the price of another investment is a derivative of that investment".

Over the past several years, the term "derivative" has been used in conjunction with a few very complicated investments that were newsworthy due to the significant losses that investors, businesses, and governments had to endure. The massive losses came about precisely because of the complexity of the offering and the fact that several factors (not to mention a few unscrupulous brokers) synchronously collided, causing major financial ruin.

Sometimes even index funds are not what they seem. In other words, do not judge a book by its cover. A classic example of this was seen in 2000. At that time, the Legg Mason Value Fund fund had the following top holdings:

	% Net Assets
America Online	7.29%
Gateway, Inc.	6.44%
UnitedHealth Group	4.80%
WorldCom	4.64%
Waste Mgmt.	4.39%
Nextel Comms Cl A	3.62%
Eastman Kodak	3.43%
WPP Group	3.40%
Citigroup	3.28%
Aetna	3.23%

Note that the word "value" appeared in the fund's name. This was very deceiving, since the top holdings were clearly weighted quite heavily toward the growth style.

Drawing another example from 2000—an odd year it seems, the Franklin Small Cap Growth Fund had over a $3 billion median market capitalization at that time. The limit for a small cap fund is usually $1 billion.

Franklin Small Cap Growth Fund - Top Holdings as of of September, 2000

Name	% Net Assets	Market Cap
JDS Uniphase	5.53%	$ 80 bill
PMC Sierra	4.17%	$ 33 bill
BEA Sys	2.44%	$ 26 bill
I2 Tech	2.27%	$ 35 bill
Veritas Software	1.90%	$ 54 bill
Micromuse	1.68%	$ 6 bill
BroadVision	1.52%	$ 8 bill
Voicestream Wireless	1.47%	$ 21 bill

Investment professionals have gone to great lengths to uncover style drift. Since it can be a tedious task, we will break it down into bite-size pieces.

First and foremost, you will need to find the most appropriate benchmark to compare the fund to. The choices are numerous, but traditional indices work best. This is because they are the standard competitors for the fund's management.

With this information in hand, you are about to become an immediate statistician. Do not panic. It is a lot easier than it seems. There are basically two different ways to do this. One is to go to www.morningstar.com or www.moneycentral.com and search for the fund that you are interested in. Then, look at the MPT statistics page and locate the R-squared calculation. If it is 80 or above, it is a good indication that it tracks its index fairly well. It is that easy!

> 📖 **MPT** (Modern Portfolio Theory)
> A comprehensive investment strategy that attempts to opti-
> mize a portfolio by measuring the relationship between risk
> and return. The risk of any investment, according to this the-
> ory, should not be viewed on its own. Rather, it should be
> considered in relation to the investment's price and the vari-
> ation of that price within the portfolio itself.

If you need more detail or if you prefer a more accurate account of the subject, you can use a spreadsheet program such as Microsoft's Excel or Google's Spreadsheets to find out if a fund is deviating from its objective. All you need to do is obtain its monthly price performance and compare it to the appropriate benchmark.

Here is the process: Navigate to the advanced charting feature on *MSN Money*. Choose the fund and then chart the daily performance for five years. Choose File>Download data, and paste the returns of the fund into a new spreadsheet in column "A." Then, do the same with the returns of the index that best matches your fund. Make certain that the data points match up. The date for the fund's return should match the index you are comparing.

Most spreadsheet programs have statistical analysis tool packs that allow you to compare two such sets of returns. Choose the correlation feature and compare the two columns of information, making sure that each uses the exact date range.

For example, in Google's Spreadsheet program, first add the data as described above. Move to a new field and then, click on the *FORMULAS* tab. On the far right of the browser window, there are choices. Click on *MORE>>*, a dropdown will appear on the screen, which has several more choices. Scroll down on the left and find *STATISTICAL*. Click it and now locate *CORREL* (correlation) and follow the online instructions. (Note: there is also an *R-squared* formula available; follow the same instructions to see if that will provide a better analysis for your data.)

If the resulting correlation is a high number (above 0.7), then your fund has accurately invested according to its charter. If, on the other hand, the correlation is lower or negative, you need to find out why. This is telling you that the manager is not sticking to his written style, as the fund's performance is not tracking its benchmark.

Tax Efficiency
It is important to understand that it is not how much you make but rather how much you keep when you invest. With that in mind, realize that mutual funds are required to pay out 90 percent of all of their earnings and gains to shareholders on an annual basis in order to keep their tax status. This status allows for the income and gains to be taxed at the shareholder level only. While traditional corporations must pay tax on earnings and then the resulting dividend is taxed to the investor (effectively doubling taxation), a mutual fund avoids this trap.

The downside for you is that you may be taxed on gains you never received. Here is how it works:

When a dividend is paid by a fund, enough shares are redeemed to cover the **distribution**. 📖

📖 DISTRIBUTION

A process where monies are paid out to shareholders. Distributions can come in the form of dividends (income from sources within the fund) or capital gains. The capital gain is either considered short- or long-term. A short-term gain is applied to sales of securities held less than 12 months, while long-term is for those held longer. The fund manager is continually buying and selling stocks or other investments within your fund, and this creates capital gains or losses. As the rule states, most of these are required to be passed on directly to shareholders.

As an investor, you may choose to either take these in cash or reinvest. If you reinvest, new shares are created and you effectively own that much more. The actual value of your holdings does not increase *or* decrease because of the distribution. The only thing that happens is the realization of a taxable event and the fund reduces the net asset value of its shares in direct proportion to the distribution.

Of course, the tax issue is only pertinent to non-qualified plans. In other words, you need not worry about this in IRAs, pensions, 40(k)s, and other tax-favored plans.

Therefore, since a high-yield bond fund provides income, it will obviously not be the most tax efficient. Equity funds, on the other hand, need to be more sensitive since they have the opportunity (and the obligation) to micromanage the tax implications of their portfolio actions.

Morningstar uses a calculation aptly named the __Morningstar__ __Tax Efficiency Ratio__,📖 which looks at past performance compared to total taxable distributions. It is a simple yet effective ratio.

> 📖   Morningstar Tax Efficiency Ratio
> This statistic, which excludes additional gains, taxes, or tax losses incurred upon selling the fund, is derived by dividing after-tax returns by pretax returns. The highest possible score would be 100 percent, which would apply to a fund that had no taxable distributions whatsoever; many municipal bond funds meet this criterion.

While it may seem that the lowest possible score would be 100 percent minus the average tax rate (roughly 60 percent), in actuality, if we assume that a fund pays out all of its total returns in distributions, a fund that pays out high income at the expense of capital gains can score even lower. This is because its taxable income distributions may actually exceed its total returns.

An equity fund with a ratio under 50 percent needs to be looked at as a possible tax nightmare. If it has more than 70 percent, it is a tax efficient fund, and it shows either a portfolio with low turnover or a manager with a good eye toward tax efficiency.

Risk Factors
Simply put, you want to pick the fund with the best return *and* the least risk. But how do you define risk and reward?

At first, you could use volatility as a guide. You could easily look at a long-term price chart to see the "ups" and "downs."

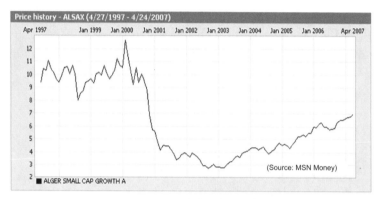

Price History of the Alger Small Cap Fund A

The problem with this method is that it is somewhat two-dimensional. It only shows the historical prices over time. You need a more accurate tool—one in which you can compare returns over time against appropriate benchmarks. This will give you a much better understanding of management's ability to perform and the risk they took to get there.

Morningstar uses a calculation that results in a **star rating**.📖

📖 THE MORNINGSTAR STAR RATING

The Morningstar risk-adjusted rating, commonly called the star rating, brings both performance and risk together into one evaluation. To determine a fund's star rating for a given period (3, 5, or 10 years), the fund's Morningstar risk score is subtracted from its Morningstar return score. The resulting number is plotted along a bell curve to determine the fund's rating for each time period.

If the fund scores in the top 10 percent of its broad investment class (domestic stock, international stock, taxable bond, or municipal bond), it receives 5 stars (highest). If it falls in the next 22.5 percent, it receives 4 stars (above average). A place in the middle 35 percent earns 3 stars (average). Those in the next 22.5 percent receive 2 stars (below average) and the bottom 10 percent get 1 star (lowest). The star ratings are recalculated monthly.

Finally, Standard & Poor's uses a **three-year overall rank**⌨ to assess risk/reward factors and then assigns a rank.

📖 THE S&P THREE-YEAR OVERALL RANK
A measure of a fund's overall risk and return characteristics. The rank is calculated using the **Sharpe Ratio.**⌨ Those funds with the highest Sharpe Ratios exhibit the best combinations of risk and return (unit of return per unit of risk) versus their peers. The rank ranges from one (lowest) to five (highest).

📖 Sharpe Ratio
A portfolio performance measure used to evaluate the return of a fund with respect to risk. The calculation is the return of the fund minus the "risk-free" rate divided by the fund's standard deviation. The Sharpe Ratio provides you with a return for unit of risk measure.

For example, assume Equity Fund 1 returned 20 percent over the past five years with a standard deviation of 2 percent. The risk-free rate is generally the interest rate on a government security. Further assume that the average return of a risk-free government bond fund over this period was 6 percent. The Sharpe Ratio would be:

$$\frac{\text{(Return of the Portfolio minus Risk-Free Rate)}}{\text{Standard Deviation of the Portfolio}}$$

In the case of Equity Fund 1, the Sharpe Ratio is (20% minus 6%) ÷ 2%, which equals 7%. Therefore, for each unit of risk, the fund returned 7% over the risk-free rate.

Generally, investors evaluating the performance of the fund would compare its Sharpe Ratio to a benchmark. This could include, but is not limited to, the average performance of similar funds or an equity index. For example, assume the S&P 500 was used as a benchmark. Further assume that the return of an S&P 500 index fund over the past five years was 10 percent with a standard deviation of 2 percent. The Sharpe Ratio for this index fund is (10% minus 6%) ÷ 2, which equals 2%.

An investor doing a side-by-side comparison between Equity Fund 1 and the S&P 500 index fund would clearly prefer Equity Fund 1, which provides a higher level of excess return for each unit of risk.

To make the fund selection process user-friendly, use the Morningstar Star System as a starting point to find quality funds. To begin with, you should look for funds with four or five stars. After your initial screen has been run, you can use other factors to refine the list of potential fund candidates.

The web address for the mutual fund screening tool is: http://moneycentral.msn.com/investor/finder/customfunds.asp.

Management Tenure

Just as it is important to stay away from relatively new funds (in existence less than three years), it makes good sense to find funds with managers that have been at the helm for a good amount of time. A minimum of four years' experience is important. This gives a good indication of how the manager has performed over time.

Since *The Disciplined Investor's* portfolio needs predictive results that can be measured over time, the management of the fund should be relatively stable. Surprisingly, you will find that this is not always the case. Attention to detail should help to confirm that there are deep roots within the fund.

Long-Term Consistency
A one-hit wonder is fine if you know precisely when to enter and exit, but the truth is that this is next to impossible. Over the years, market timers have provided us with enough bad calls to teach us this basic fact.

A better move is to look for funds and managers that have seen both good and bad markets and have performed well over time. Since historical information is a tool not to be used as a projection device, the best use you can make of it is to understand the management's basic methods and skills.

After the basic management screens have been completed, check the fund against both its peers and its assigned benchmark. By finding those managers who have outperformed over the long haul, you are apt to gain the benefit of their wisdom. Look especially closely at the years in which their benchmark was down. How did this fund perform? Was it hurt just as badly? During those periods of decline, did the manager provide a value-added benefit and in so doing, save his investors significant financial losses?

Both 5 and 10 years of history should be sufficient to help you discern a manager's strengths and weaknesses. The more history a fund has, the better.

Relevance

Taking all of the reports provided by both Morningstar and *MSN Money* into consideration, it is easy to see that there are many statistics available. But beware. Not all of the numbers presented are applicable to every fund.

For example, some funds have low correlation, or similarity of historical returns, to their benchmark. If this is true, you should find that the R-squared is usually low. In this case, when pondering the statistical information, it may look initially as if the fund measures up, but you must realize that the statistics may bear no relevance. In other words, it may quite possibly be unusable information.

Sometimes, the information can be confounding. Sizing up a fund that carries a low R-squared is something like answering the question, "Would you rather take your lunch or walk to school?" There are two items presented with no comparative significance. Exactly for that reason, look to other items such as raw volatility, associated fees, and relative versus actual performance.

If the R-squared is higher than 80, many of the MPT risk tools can be of real benefit in trying to understand the fund. Sharpe ratios as well as other MPT (modern portfolio theory) analytics can be invaluable in the research process.

In summary, using the *MSN Money* fund screening and finder tool is an excellent way for you to narrow the universe of funds. By doing so, you use a powerful mechanism with data updated on a regular basis. This in itself is important, as funds can change management and overall style with regularity. As a *Disciplined Investor*, you can stay ahead of the curve by creating tested and reusable systems in an attempt to gain superior overall returns with less overall risk.

The funds chosen should be monitored regularly, with an eye toward relative performance against appropriate peers and benchmarks. Keep in mind that a significant market event can temporarily undermine any portfolio. This is the main reason why adherence to a plan is so important when investing. Unless there has been a significant change in management style or other important issues pertaining to the fund structure, be patient and stay with your well-researched choices.

Summarizing the points made above, you could say that you are on a hunt for excellence. You should seek out funds with superior results that have less risk and limited cost. The good news is that there are so many fine choices available that finding the right fund to meet your investment objectives should be easier with these freely available tools and adherence to the system standards. It will take practice and patience, and it will involve a little bit of work on your part. But yes, you *can* do it yourself.

The end result should allow for maintained consistency; the essential byproduct of a discipline. By staying close to the disciplines outlined, you will be able to make better choices about mutual funds and have a good idea of the exact performance expectations once they are implemented.

Additional Considerations:

Fund Value/Growth Indicator:

Price/Earnings Ratio	Style	Price/Book Ratio
Over 19	Growth	Over 4.5
Under 19	Value	Under 4.5

Fund Capitalization Indicator:

Size Indicator	Median Market Cap
Large-cap	$5 billion+
Mid-cap	$1 – $5 billion
Small-cap	$500 million – $1 billion
Micro-cap	Under $500 million

Now that the significance of mutual funds has been established, it would best serve the cause to move on to another avenue of disciplined investing. In any comprehensive approach to building a balanced portfolio, a discussion of annuities and guaranteed investment contracts is certainly warranted.

While mutual funds represent a much easier and steadier method of diversification—and are relatively new in form and function—annuities and guaranteed investment contracts have been around for centuries. Some investors may view such methods as perhaps a little outdated, but annuities and guaranteed investment contracts have been around so long for a reason: they work.

Throughout a long and tumultuous financial history that saw the rise and fall of empires and the Dow Jones Industrial Average, annuities and GICs have remained steadfast, offering a heightened sense of security and safety for all those saving for their future.

And what of retirement? Even if it may seem like a distant condition—something that is still too far off in your life to even consider—an annuity or GICs may have its valuable applications in your own portfolio. They may not be as versatile as they are old, but you would still do well to take a good long look. The following chapter does just that.

Chapter 7

Annuities and GICs

Annuities and guaranteed investment contracts (GICs) have long been tools used by savvy investors to help reduce risk within their portfolios. Before there was the S&P 500 or theories based on the Dow Jones Industrials, guaranteed investment contracts were a large part of most individuals' long-term retirement plans. They offered safety, guarantees, and freedom from the fear of running out of money.

These programs have a long history, tracing their roots as far back as the Roman Empire in the 700s. Unfortunately, though, with the lack of in-depth knowledge on the part of many agents (along with a significant amount of bad press) most good annuities have not seen the benefit of reaching the investment masses. Add to that the fact that the lack of an appealing interest rate does nothing to inspire investors to seek out annuities as core components within their portfolios, and what you are left with is a thoroughly underrated investment strategy.

If you jump ahead to the final chapter and its section on asset allocation, you may begin to realize that much of that was essentially developed to reduce risk and, at the same time, increase return. Annuities, it may be said, represent just one more method to help you gain control over the risk associated with your portfolio.

On the complete opposite side of the traditional risk spectrum, guaranteed investment contracts (GICs) also referred to as "*fixed annuities*," allow for absolute guarantees—along with an understanding about and the expectation of the future value of the investment in question.

Annuities have seen many changes over time, and in 1995 there was a major shift in policy design that allowed for insurance companies to compete with more traditional investments. Fixed annuities were now not only based on a static interest rate declared by the insurance company; their performance would also be dynamically affected by the returns of the stock markets. The idea of an "Equity Index Annuity" was born out of the need for companies to become more competitive with the rapidly changing investment climate.

Yet it was only after the year 2000 that annuities once again started to gain popularity. As investment portfolios continued to hemorrhage due to a market that seemed to move lower daily, investors became more and more open to new ideas about how to recapture their money. Those new ideas carried a natural bend toward conservatism.

Unfortunately, most investors in this country failed to take action until much of their wealth had already been stripped away by the volatility of the economy at the turn of the 21st century. By the time they became receptive to the alternatives, it was almost too late.

Perhaps a dash of historical perspective will shed some light on this often confusing topic. Records show that the first reported annuities date back to Roman times, when contracts known as "annua" were first offered. They consisted of a promise of income payments for a fixed term—possibly even a life term—to an individual investor in return for the deposit of a sum of money. Back then, speculators were the main source of offerings for these types of contracts when they provided insurance to marine and other risky enterprises.

The first person to understand calculations and tables that recorded life expectancies was a Roman named Domitius Ulpianus. His main objective was to use it for the purpose of calculating income rights for his descendants.

It was not until the middle ages, however, that annuities were first made available to individuals who wished to deposit large sums of money. Later still, during the 17th century, special annuity programs that pooled the assets of many people had begun operation in France and Europe. These programs were known as **Tontines**.📖

📖   TONTINE
An investment plan in which participants buy shares in a common fund and receive an annuity that increases every time a participant dies—with the entire fund going to the final survivor or to those who survive after a specified period of time.

In return for the promise of an initial lump sum payment, purchasers of tontines received life annuities. Annuity payments would increase annually for the survivors who remained. They would then claim the payouts which would have gone to those who had died. When only one survivor of the tontine pool was left, he or she would get the entire principal in a lump sum.

The tontine had elements of both gambling and insurance tied together in a neat package. It also caused a great deal of legal and social concern as the financial gain of one participant was so closely tied to the life and death of others.

During the same period, there were many nations that turned to selling annuities in lieu of government bonds. History shows that it was initially England and Holland that had programs in which annuity companies received investment funds in return for the promise to pay annuitants a lifetime income.

By the year 1759, the United States entered the fray, seeing for the first time the initial availability of annuities for individuals. The first annuity has been credited to the design of *The Corporation for the Relief of Poor and Distressed Presbyterian Ministers and Distressed Widows and Children's Ministers*, a company that was chartered by the state of Pennsylvania. This organization provided survivorship annuities for families as well as ministers. As an exclusive organization that took care of its members, it was credited with creating one of the first forms of guaranteed income. In fact, it eventually paved the way for other companies that later devised programs for anyone who wished to receive such guarantees.

A half century later another company, *The Pennsylvania Company for Insurance on Lives and Granting Annuities*, was founded. The annuity market was not in high demand at the time since life expectancies were not very long. Therefore growth of the company was slow, but this company can be said to have founded what is today the modern stock insurance company. More importantly, they were one of the first companies to ever sell annuities and life insurance directly to the public without a membership requirement.

Over the course of the past century, there has been a dramatic shift on the part of the public toward annuities as an alternative to guaranteed investment contracts. For a long time, this movement was dominated by investments in sovereign bonds and programs from banking-related institutions. As investments became more diverse, so did the plans offered by annuity companies.

Today the product range has changed in such a way that the offerings can provide more than just guaranteed incomes. They also represent opportunities for deferral of income taxation until the individual decides to withdraw the money.

Within this chapter, you will learn about the advantages of some of the more "modern" annuities that provide an investor with a better mix of allocation options, thereby reducing risk and minimizing the long-term volatility within a portfolio. Taxation and the details regarding some of the more obscure types of annuities (two topics which would fill a book by themselves) will not be discussed in any significant length within these pages.

Realize that annuities come in many sizes and shapes, but for the most part, they can be broken down into two separate subdivisions. Within the subdivisions, there are also many different categories that can be further refined along the lines of how the annuity in question relates to and may benefit a port-folio, the length of time required to hold the contract, and whether you plan to postpone the investment return or wish to receive it immediately.

For the purposes of this chapter, think about the universe of annuities as though it were split into two distinct sections: the galaxy of fixed annuities and the galaxy of variable annu-ities. These two distinct areas are differentiated by the underlying investments within their respective annuities. The level of guarantee that is offered to the purchaser of the plan is also considered a dividing factor.

With a fixed annuity, you will have the guarantee of prin-cipal and usually some stated return for a specified period of time. On the opposite side of this is the variable annuity, which offers a wide array of investment choices within an insurance/annuity wrapper. There are traditionally no specific guarantees within the investment accounts, and the owner must be willing to accept the risk of principal fluctuation as well as the potential for loss.

To make this distinction crystal clear: a fixed annuity allows you to completely eliminate the risk of investment loss within the plan and transfer it to the insurance company. With a variable annuity, the risk of loss is passed on to the contract holder. The latter is the reason why variable annuities are often favorably compared to investments in mutual funds, as they have the added features of tax deferral and death benefits.

Variable Annuities
Since the stated goal of this chapter is to help you further diversify and reduce risk, discussions of variable annuities will

be purposely limited to a few comparisons and a cursory review of the programs available.

Variable annuities can be said to be the marriage of investments and insurance. During the annuity accumulation phase it is quite similar to any investment. Funds are deposited into accounts that closely resemble mutual funds. The units within the variable annuity accounts are calculated similar to shares of mutual funds.

That is where the similarities between variable annuities and investments end, and the differences begin. One major differentiation is that there are no dividends, capital gains distributions, or interest payments within the variable annuity sub-accounts. Even though the investments within these accounts will have distributions, the variable annuity will reinvest them internally. In fact, it will be unnoticeable to the annuity holder, as it occurs automatically. The only thing that may happen is the account shares may move in proportion to the reinvestment. This will only be seen if you compare the variable annuity sub-account to the mutual fund it is patterned after on the day of the distribution.

Even with this advanced knowledge, it will be very difficult to detect. Why bother anyway? Remember that a deferred variable annuity is often purchased as a tax-advantaged investment vehicle for which the lack of immediate income distributions is of no consequence to most investors.

Drawing from the textbook definition of a variable annuity, when the accumulation phase of the annuity ends, the cumulative value of the investment units are transformed or converted into "annuity units." This occurs as if the underlying unit values were distributed and the funds would have bought a hypothetical fixed annuity.

While there is no actual payment to the annuitant, the values are important when calculating income for the future. The calculated amount is used to provide the actual annuity with the appropriate number of annuity units. This, in turn, is used to provide the annuitant with realistic projections of future values; that way, the investor can choose which option is most appropriate for his or her particular situation.

Many variable annuities also allow the annuitant the option of choosing a fixed annuity stream or some combination of a fixed and variable stream of payouts. In practice, most people seem to choose a variable annuity for growth, and when they are ready for income, they move to a fixed style to ensure that they will never run out of money.

To confuse the situation just a bit more, the variable annuity payout depends on the number of annuity units with which the annuitant is credited due to net deposits. Over time, the actual returns on the assets in the portfolio underlying variable annuities also affect the total payout.

For that reason, a variable payout is a double-edged sword. It can provide a wonderful hedge against inflation, but it may also bring uncertainty to a retiree's annual budget. This is due to the fact that as the value of the underlying portfolio rises, the income will also rise during the payout phase. Thus it can be said that a variable annuity is a great tool to keep the purchasing power of a portfolio stable.

Unfortunately, though, the converse is also true. The value of the annuity portfolio will dictate the amount of income generated. If the annuity value declines, future payments will decline as well. The opportunity to earn money is beneficial but at the same time can lead to problems. Therefore a variable annuity has the potential for fluctuating payments.

Over time, many product incarnations have been devised. There are now a plethora of options available, as the market for this type of annuities has become more competitive. The biggest change has been in the number of investment alternatives that are available within a variable annuity. While the first variable annuities focused primarily on diversified common stock portfolios, many of the plans today offer more specialized portfolios of stocks and indices (as well as bonds and other non-traditional securities).

By their nature, variable annuities allow policyholders to switch between sub-accounts in order to change investment allocations (usually with different investment options and objectives). Therefore it is possible to move from one "fund family" or "style" to another without the traditional expense and delay. This is usually done without fees or penalties, although there may be a limit on the number of annual transfers allowed by contract.

These features make it possible to choose variable annuities as a viable accumulation vehicle without necessarily requiring you to purchase annuity-like payouts until the accumulation phase is over. Add to that the fact that many contracts contain purchase rate guarantees, and therein lies a terrific avenue for investing without risk.

Without risk? What does that mean?

The insurance component of a variable annuity states that upon the death of the annuitant, the contract will equal *at least* the net deposits (deposits minus withdrawals). Therefore, if an investor deposits $100,000 into a variable annuity and the value of its underlying investments falls below the original amount deposited, the value of the "death benefit" will be equal to the net deposits.

This particular component is obviously very attractive to many investors, especially older individuals who want to protect their assets without handcuffing themselves to CDs and money markets.

Since, in this scenario, the beneficiaries will never receive less than the net deposit, an investor could theoretically create an aggressive portfolio attempting to maximize gain. At the same time, he could rest easy knowing that upon his death, his heirs are assured that the value of the annuity would never be less than the sum of the deposits, less any withdrawals.

Insurers offer a range of different annuity products that compete in turn with a range of financial products offered by other financial institutions. The variable annuity is the insurance company's closest relative to the traditional mutual fund, with a few distinct differences. The first is an increased annual cost. The second is the potential penalty on early withdrawals that will be assessed by the annuity company. Finally, there is traditionally a minimum age requirement of $59\frac{1}{2}$ set by the IRS for withdrawing money without a penalty.

These are the trade-offs required to obtain the death benefit and built-in tax deferral. So, you may find yourself asking, "How much will these actually cost?" The total cost of ownership of the annuity includes the underlying investment manager fees as well as mortality and expense charges. These may total anywhere from two to four percent per year, depending on the company.

Unlike other financial products, annuities usually contain a **surrender charge**.📖 This is found in many deferred annuity contracts as part of the initial agreement between the buyer and the annuity company. Basically, if an annuitant decides to cancel his policy before the end of the stated **surrender period**,📖 he will be required to forfeit some of his account value to the insurer in the form of a surrender charge.

This concept is quite similar to the contingent deferred sales charges associated with mutual funds. The justification by the insurer is that these charges are required in order to recover the commission and other production and distribution costs associated with the annuity. Their profit model states that the longer the money is held within the annuity policy, the more expenses the insurance company can recoup. This is all part of the annual administration and mortality fees assessed.

However, if the annuity is terminated prematurely, the amount collected will be insufficient to allow for the recapturing of these fees. Therefore, the insurer deems it appropriate to collect the surrender charge in order to be repaid for the loss.

📖 SURRENDER CHARGE
A fee imposed upon an investor who decides to prematurely terminate an annuity contract. The charge is usually higher during the early years of the surrender period (see below)

and then gradually declines by a certain percentage each year. Some companies offer annuities without these charges and are considered "no-load" annuities.

📖 SURRENDER PERIOD
The period of time under which a surrender charge applies to the sale of, or withdrawal from, an annuity. Typically, this period is somewhere between seven to nine years. If an investor decides to sell all or part of an annuity early (such as during this pre-established period of time), he is subject to the surrender charge—based on the percentage associated with the specific year of the surrender period in which the sell or withdrawal is enacted.

The IRS has a hand in this as well. As annuities are created as tax deferred vehicles, the IRS can impose a tax penalty on early distributions. When this is added to the potential surrender charges on early withdrawals, one quickly realizes that annuities are not for the short-term investor who has not yet reached the age of 59½. Still, the tax treatment of annuities is an attractive feature that seems to have been a significant catalyst for their recent growth in popularity. This is because growth on the investments held within a deferred annuity account is not subject to taxation until it is withdrawn from the plan. As we know, when monies are allowed to compound over long periods of time unhindered by income or capital gains taxes, there is a wonderful opportunity for exponential growth.

The significant opportunity to defer taxes on the investments held within an annuity has already been discussed at length, but here is a final illustration of the points discussed to hammer this home:

Assume that a 45-year-old with a projected retirement age of 70 is looking at various investment opportunities in order to fund his eventual retirement. He and his financial planner use a return expectation of 7 percent year over year and a 28 percent marginal tax rate for his $25,000 initial investment.

Under these assumptions, the $25,000 investment *outside* of an annuity would grow to a bit over $85,000 by the time the investor reached 70. This is assuming that each year 28 percent of the income generated is deducted for taxes and the remainder is reinvested.

Now, look at the same $25,000 invested *inside* of an annuity. The assumptions are all the same except that the annuity gains are tax deferred. Here, the principal would accumulate to more than $135,000 by the time the investor turned 70. The marginal 28 percent tax rate has been assumed in this case as well. Once he decided to withdraw the funds from his annuity, he would find that the remaining after-tax value would equal $97,693.

The amount above represents a 15 percent increase in profit over the amount within the non-annuity investment. Suffice it to say that a variable annuity is an extremely efficient way to save for retirement and works nicely as a compliment to standard retirement programs such as IRAs, pension plans, and 401(k) plans. But, there is one more hidden expense that needs to be discussed again before we all rejoice and buy up the entire supply of annuity contracts. Earlier, we explored the cost factors of an annuity and found that the variable annuity has an additional annual cost related to mortality and administration expenses. If that is included in the same equation, the annuity may not perform as well as first thought.

All assumptions being equal, the additional annual expenses (1% assumed) would bring the final after-tax value of the annuity closer to $84,253. This particular point is one that is often overlooked when purchasing a variable annuity. The lesson to be learned, once again, is that all costs should be taken into consideration when researching any investment. If, after a thorough review of this chapter, it still makes sense to invest in a variable annuity, look for a plan with a low-cost structure or the tax benefits you receive will only offset the additional costs you will pay.

This poignant discussion is leading toward the reason that, in the mid-1990s, an annuity design was introduced which gained tremendous popularity: the index annuity. Up until then, individuals had only two choices when it came to annuities: fixed annuities offering a guaranteed rate and variable annuities with "mutual-fund-like" sub-accounts. As more investors became disillusioned with the performance results of their variable annuities, annuity companies looked to provide more guarantees. At the same time, investors were still desirous of investing in the markets. The blending of these helped to give birth to an annuity that would have characteristics of both variable and fixed annuities.

One component of this new type of annuity was to provide a low-cost structure in order to compete with variable annuities. The mortality and administration expenses were removed and replaced with caps, spreads, and participation rates. These had the ability to ensure profits to the annuity company while allowing the investor to capture some of the market's gains.

The basic premise of an index annuity is to provide returns that are similar to many common equity and fixed-income indices such as S&P 500, NASDAQ 100, Lehman Bond, or the DJIA. The attraction to this type of plan is that investors can have returns tied to the changes in the general markets while still maintaining a degree of safety. Unfortunately though, the calculation of the returns is not always straightforward, as they usually contain a few confusing statistical measures. For example, issuers of index annuities always specify the level at which index annuity owners will be "in the market." This level is called the **participation rate**, 📖 and it reflects how closely the annuity follows the index's performance.

📖　PARTICIPATION RATE

This rate is quoted in terms of a percentage. Suppose an index annuity has a defined participation rate of 70 percent. When the index it follows goes up by 10 percent, the annuity's accumulated value increases by 7 percent. In a market downturn, an insurance company mitigates the risk. Participation rates of 80, 90, or 100 percent are typical, and it is important to ensure this rate is guaranteed throughout the term of the annuity.

In order to mitigate the risk of excessive interest payments due on an annuity, some annuity policies may utilize a **spread**. 📖 The main reason for this is to ensure profitability for the insurance company.

📖　SPREAD

The spread is the difference between what an annuity fund actually earns and the amount that is credited to the investor.

Spreads or fees are not a new idea. In fact, they are not restricted to annuities either. Whenever you open a savings account, for example, you are subject to a spread. The bank may be earning five percent on your money, but in a savings account, they are only paying you two percent. In this example, the three percent difference is the spread.

In the case of index annuities, the annual spread can range anywhere from zero to five percent and is clearly reflected both in the initial contract and on the annual statements issued by the insurer. Some contracts do not have a spread at all, which will usually be guaranteed in the contract terms.

As with any annuity, index annuities are subject to a 10 percent penalty by the IRS for any premature withdrawal of earnings made by an annuitant under the age of 59½. Also, excessive withdrawals made before the index annuity matures will sometimes incur penalties imposed by the annuity company.

Most insurers, though, will allow a certain amount to be withdrawn every year without penalty. Some even allow free withdrawals for qualifying events such as a nursing home emergency.

With the surge in popularity of index annuities, more insurance companies have designed programs with wide-ranging options. As a result, picking and choosing the right index annuity can sometimes be a difficult decision.

To help you sort through the confusion surrounding index and variable annuities, the next two pages provide a checklist to help assist when selecting the annuity that is right for you.

Strong Ratings

What kind of assurances and guarantees does the company make? Ensure that it will be around when you need it most. Look for insurance company ratings of "A" (excellent) or better.

Spreads or Fees vs. Caps

A spread is a fee that is subtracted from an index return after applying the participation rate. It is usually declared and guaranteed for a period of one year or more. A cap, on the other hand, is a limit put on an index return after applying the participation rate. It is also usually set and guaranteed for a period of one year or more.

Participation Rates

Higher participation rates are usually better. However, higher spreads or lower caps can reduce the benefits of a higher participation rate. Make sure you read the fine print.

Surrender Period

Index annuities typically have longer maturities than other annuities. Make sure that the surrender period lasts no longer than 10 to 12 years. Shorter surrender periods are available.

Free Withdrawals

Most companies offer withdrawal of 10 percent of your original annuity's value every year, free of penalty. However, you should look for a company that offers a 10 percent withdrawal on the accumulated value, not the invested amount.

Nursing Home Waivers

Some index annuities allow you to pull out additional money, penalty free, if you are confined to a hospital or nursing home. The usual standard is 90 days of confinement to qualify for the free withdrawal. If you do not own long-term care protection, this could be an important factor.

Death Benefits

Some contracts provide instant liquidity should the annuity owner or annuitant die before the contract has matured. Make sure your contract provides either the accumulated value (pre-ferred value) or the surrender value, and that the contract *does not* need to continue to the completion of the annuity term in order to withdraw your entire lump sum value.

Indexing Period

Does your annuity track index changes annually on a monthly average basis or on a point-to-point basis?

Annuitization Options

What options does the index annuity provide for withdrawing money? Make sure you have good options to choose from, including the option *not* to annuitize in order to access your money when the term is complete. Annuitization is often not recommended.

High-powered though they may seem, certain variable and index annuities should not be mistaken for the only necessary answer to your portfolio needs. They are merely *general* ways to help reduce risk. In no way should they be considered anything more than small parts of a *Disciplined Investor's* portfolio.

Since this chapter (and the chapter that precedes it) merely outlines a supplemental investment strategy, you may find a great deal more advice to help round things out in Chapter 9.

Now that you have been exposed to several underlying methods of achieving a disciplined investment portfolio, it is prudent to study *how* to go about the act of investing.

There are many levels of action that you can take. From the intrepid investor who feels no need to seek outside advice to the casual investor who would rather have a financial advisor or certified financial planner handle his or her portfolio, there is something out there for everyone. Thanks to this Internet-powered world of communication that we now live in, there are plenty of options at hand to help you to discover how to invest. Regardless of what your situation is, the next two chapters aim to help you find your niche.

Chapter 8

Tools of the Trade

How about the do-it-yourself investor inside all of us? Perhaps you cannot imagine finding anyone more capable of handling your money than you are. Maybe you are a retiree with more extra time on your hands than you would care to think about. Or, it could be that you do not feel that financial advisors are trustworthy enough to manage your portfolio.

If your feelings are similar to any of these descriptions, take heart in the fact that there is a whole host of consumer-driven toolsets available to the hands-on user such as yourself. Whether you prefer to get your information in the more traditional vein (via periodicals, magazines, or books) or focus on the cutting edge of market technology (user-friendly websites, self-directed trading firms, and up-to-the-second news and trend updates), there is something out there for you.

In this chapter, you will be provided with a semi-comprehensive guide to navigating the treacherous and sometimes costly waters of investment-oriented tools on the market.

The key to finding success in personal investing is to employ a well-balanced attack. With so many options, aids, and sources of information to choose from, this is no simple task. The prospect of absorbing the many ins-and-outs of the investment industry on a daily basis can be an incredibly overwhelming undertaking.

Because of this, it is easy to get sucked into a narrow-minded approach to personal investing. Make no mistake: if your goal is to see higher, steadier, and quicker returns on your money, you will need to get your information from the widest array of sources possible.

The marketplace has a tremendous number of investment strategy tools available. Some are worth your time and some are not. Fortunately, there are many that are high quality, which will make your task of well-informed investing much simpler. The goal is to separate the good from the bad. In this chapter, you will find that it has been done for you. The list below sums up six different categories of personal investment tools that will be discussed:

The Six Essential Tools for *The Disciplined Investor*:
- "Easy" Stock-Selection Programs
- Online and Print News Forums
- Online Personal Finance Services
- Web- and Desktop-Based Informational Tools
- Self-Directed Brokerage Firms
- Money-Management Software

"Easy" Stock-Selection Programs
The word "easy" in this subject header is in quotations for a good reason. Stock-selection tools and red-green, buy-sell engines that you may have seen on TV are usually not as easy to use as the advertisements would lead you to believe. These

are sometimes referred to as "black box" systems, as their inner workings are usually a mystery.

Some of these tools may be moderately effective guides for *when* to buy and sell, though they are less effective at explaining *how* to buy and sell. This is an important distinction to make because, as has been stressed again and again, action without reason very rarely leads to a healthy return on an investment.

It *is* possible that these programs may work for some investors. There are a great many success stories that come with the territory, but there are also many horror stories that suggest a level of difficulty and frustration that is less than appealing to most users. Nothing is easy in investing. Thinking otherwise can be more damaging than you realize.

The other point to remember about "black box" programs is that there are often substantial risks involved with putting all your stock (no pun intended) in a supposedly standalone product. If it were really so easy that anyone could do it, *everyone* would be doing it.

These tools may be perfectly acceptable if you plan to use them to enhance a few of the more traditional trading and investment disciplines. Their ease-of-use claims however, should *rarely* be taken at face value. Remember, if it seems too good to be true, it probably is.

The final downfall of these programs comes with the fee structure. While they may carry an attractive up-front price tag, in the long run they almost always wind up costing the end-user a great deal more than they bargained for. With all the paper-trading training, highly recommended seminars, for-fee stock-tips, and other add-ons peddled by these programs, by day's end you will be amazed at just how much money you have spent on making "easy" money.

Online and Print News Forums

If you are a self-directed investor in search of a supposedly unbiased news source for market trends, stock tips, and penny-edition advisory strategies, you probably know that there is certainly no shortage of material available both online and in print. The trouble with so much quantity, however, is that it so often dilutes quality. It is like trying to take a sip of water from an open fire hydrant.

The most important thing to consider when sizing up the many sources for investment-related news is *where* the information is coming from.

For instance, while it is crucial to read some kind of morning-edition newspaper—they provide an excellent foundation for the knowledgeable investor—some small-market papers may not be the most appropriate sources for financial news. It's not that they attempt to mislead their readers. In some cases it may be that they do not employ a large enough staff to offer the variety of opinions that it takes to provide a comprehensive look at the markets.

If you are the kind of investor who fears turning over your money to the control of a financial advisor, you have something to consider. If you have been basing your buy-and-sell decisions on the advice from your local paper's business section, realize you may have been putting your trust in only one person's opinion. The second issue that should be considered is the potential biases that the source in question may carry.

If you are a dedicated reader of any of the money-related magazines, then you must pass everything you read through an "advertising filter." In other words, ask yourself how much of the content of each story is dedicated to lauding the same companies that advertise within the periodical. How many of their "Top Lists," such as the ones for stocks or mutual funds, include at least one or two of their most prominent advertising clients? Remember, magazines have to make money too, and there is a lot of money to be made in selling ad space.

None of this is intended to scare you away from online and print news in general. If you want to find success as a self-driven investor, you absolutely must dedicate a sensible portion of your time to learning all you can about the market and its trends. Find a thorough and reliable source for daily news and read it each morning; spend some time on the week-end catching up on the trends highlighted in a reliable periodical or magazine. Later in this chapter, you will find top picks for the most unbiased sources of market news.

Online Personal Finance Services
There are many online services out there—supposedly comprehensive websites that supply all the materials needed to make well-informed investment decisions—but only a select few stack up to *The Disciplined Investor's* standards.

There are many sites to help research and track stocks and bonds, manage personal savings, plan for retirement, balance the checkbook, and boost a waning credit score, all in one place. Does that seem too good to be true? Surprisingly, you can find all of these services and more on a few key websites as long as you are willing to spend a good portion of your day in front of the computer. For many, these tools are more than enough to provide a solid foundation for managing their own portfolio.

There are a few items to examine about an online personal finance service before taking the time to set up a user account. The first thing you should do is explore the website's interface and features. While there are several qualified services out there, some of them are a bit more user-friendly and sensibly designed than others. There is really nothing more annoying and (sometimes) time-consuming than having to struggle through the confusing navigation of a poorly designed website. It would really be a shame to get in on an investment a moment too late just because you could not gain access to the information you needed quickly enough.

The second thing you should consider is how much each service costs. While the majority of these providers boast free access to their all-encompassing online software, not many of them follow through on that claim. More often than not, you will find yourself signing up for a rather bareboned product and then regularly subjected to up-selling strategies. If an online personal finance provider advertises a tiered service structure, avoid it at all costs.

Lastly, you must consider how and where the service provider in question gets its information. Typically, it will be allied with one of the more prominent news sources available, but how does it go about gathering information and how quick is it to update it? If you have all the tools to make your investment decisions but have outdated information on which to base those decisions, what good are the tools in the first place?

It should also be noted here that when the term "outdated information" is mentioned these days, it refers to any data that is more than 10 seconds old.

Fortunately there are at least a few qualified online personal finance services floating around in the ocean known as the web. Later in the chapter you will find a list of those that provide excellent services to *Disciplined Investors*.

Web- and Desktop-Based Informational Tools
Which of these do you need? How much is too much? What is it all about, anyway?

The answer to the last question is simple: apart from those offered within the online personal finance services discussed above, it is plainly about the many standalone market and investment-related tools available to the savvy investor.

There are services that provide up-to-date charts on market trends and tendencies. There are always-on tools to track your favorite stocks without even opening your web browser. There are programs that alert you when, for example, your stocks are approaching their sell stops or 52-week highs. If you are looking for no-hassle, easily accessible information, there is certainly no shortage of sources on which to report.

How much is too much? There is a happy medium, to be certain. While it is important to maintain exactly the kind of information you need, it is also important to avoid bogging yourself down with informational-tool overload. Many of the stats, charts, and graphs are little more than bells and whistles anyway. Again, with all of the options available, an important factor to consider is the cost of each service in question.

Which tools do you need? If your goal is to light up your computer's desktop like a Christmas tree, then go ahead and Google the phrase, "investment tools" and start downloading. If, on the other hand, you are looking for value-added tools to assist in the implementation of your investment strategy, then there are only a few that you should consider.

Self-Directed Brokerage Firms
Like all of the toolsets listed above, there are many qualified providers within this arena listed at the end of this chapter. The truly interesting thing about these companies is that their concept, in itself, is a bit of a paradox. As an online investment firm, it is difficult to advertise that your customers are truly self-directed while still touting (and charging for) advisory services.

In addition, firms that fall under this category often tend to quote low per-trade fees. The trouble with this concept is that the trading fees are often just the tip of the iceberg. Even so, at their core is something quite valuable, even for the most independent-minded investor.

As online money-management tools, they function much like Internet bank accounts. In other words, they facilitate comprehensive access to all of your funds and assets, which, at the very least, should make your life that much easier. Also, it should be noted that if something were to happen to you, gathering and managing your portfolio on the part of your trust manager, attorney, or heirs would be greatly simplified.

As with most products and services, not all self-directed brokerage firms are created equally. Some may have excellent customer service but poor presentation and clunky navigation.

Others may boast a completely user-friendly interface while silently providing completely inaccurate information. Still others may ignore the self-directed aspect of the company mission and try to up-sell you at every turn.

While all of these scenarios can occur, there are still many benefits to adding a firm from this category to your balanced investment approach. There is no service on the Internet better equipped to help you manage and track the brokerage aspect of your portfolio than an online brokerage firm. For a variety of reasons, however, some of these companies are better than others. Actors like Sam Waterston may be charismatic, but not everything he says on TV should be taken as pure gospel. In response, several of the biggest companies are reviewed toward the end of this chapter and the pros and cons of each are summarized.

Money-Management Software

There was a time, not too long ago, when you could find software for just about anything. These days, though, the software section in the nearest electronics store seems to shrink by a shelf or two every month.

There are a few reasons for this. First, it's a lot more cost-effective for a software company to provide their product online, rather than "out of the box." Second, more and more people are turning to the web to meet their everyday service needs. And, finally, the Internet is simply a much safer place in which to do business than it was 10 years ago.

Once upon a time, desktop-based software was more attractive to the discerning user because of fears over Internet security. It simply was not safe to keep or transmit your personal information on a network. Things are changing quickly, however. Gone are the days when the Internet was little more than a thief-laden jungle where no transaction was truly secure.

In short, traditional software platforms are becoming obsolete. Why put Quicken on your desktop and spend the time to sync it to your online account when you can just access everything at the Quicken website anyway?

While the future of the industry may see these platforms headed out the door, since they are still available today they are worth mentioning. The fact is that they will continue to form an integral part of the balanced investment attack. There are few things easier than graphing your profits and losses or balancing your checkbook on the computer anyway.

The Balanced Plan

Before outlining the basic tenets of the recommended tools for supplementing your investment strategies, it might be beneficial to provide a cautionary tale of computer-based investing failure—a kind of "what not to do" for the self-driven investor.

Take as an example a fine fellow named Steve. To begin with, Steve's first mistake was taking an all-too-narrow approach to his stock trading.

Steve, like so many self-driven investors, was drawn in by the allure of an easy-to-use, get-rich-quick kind of system. He was sold on the red and green flashing lights of what will be called the StockLights.com program (a fictitious company/system). This software vendor suggests that all one needs to do in order to beat the markets is have a visual aid that indicates buying and selling points. It comes with a sorely lacking and probably overly biased support structure consisting of user groups and so-called experts. Many of these systems have only a rudimentary understanding of the many facets of the stock trading process.

What's more, StockLights.com boasted that it was so confident in its program it was even willing to offer Steve (like all unsuspecting customers) the opportunity to try it out before he committed to paying for it.

So, in the beginning, Steve decided to play it safe. He researched the software, kicked its tires a little, and signed up for the trial program. He plugged in a few of his favorite stocks and watched as the red, green, and yellow signals dictated his would-be actions. StockLights.com provided him with message boards, stock "calls," and tips of the day, and he felt confident that it equipped him with an insider's knowledge of how to buy and sell his way into riches. The program seemed to be working—and working well.

What little doubt Steve had was quickly melted away when he made thousands of pretend dollars per month in paper trading. He paid to learn how to use the so-called brilliant software to manipulate the markets to his advantage and literally rake in the money along the way.

The only trouble is that trading with Monopoly money is very different than trading with real money. When faced with the prospect of losing something substantial, and when gambling on real companies that make rather less-predictable moves, people tend to behave quite differently than when trading in a consequence-free bubble. They sell too early. They buy too big. They just do not carry the kind of patience and limited emotion it takes to play the markets on carefully calculated information rather than gut feelings.

When Steve made the move from paper trading to real-world, live trading, he lost his shirt. He went from making $30,000 pretend dollars per month to losing close to $60,000 almost immediately. To add insult, he had not only wasted all that money buying the program, but there were also the fees associated with all of the add-ons and considerable hidden costs that came along with the service.

What Steve failed to realize was that when approaching investing on one's own, the best plan of attack is a versatile one. In this case, the StockLights.com "package" was simply too narrow. While the essential elements of a successful plan may have been there—the program offered a low-cost tracking tool, charting services, and supposedly unbiased information to supplement a user's market knowledge—in the end Steve's approach was just too shallow and one-dimensional. All of his information and support came from a single source that, as it turned out, was not the most reliable one available to him.

A better strategy for Steve would have been threefold. First, he should have more appropriately assessed his comfort level in taking on the responsibility of managing his own investing. Steve, being the kind of person who would rather buy into a program that offered an easy way to make money than put in the time and effort it would take to truly invest in the markets well, probably would have been better served to seek the advice of an advisor in the first place.

Second, he should have done his homework—in other words, sought alternative sources from which to gather information. Considering the fact that he had no idea just where the StockLights.com tips were coming from, there was no way for him to tell the difference between sound advice and that designed to benefit the interests of the tipsters themselves.

Third, Steve should have worked to build a balanced plan that did not rely so heavily on one specific investing tool. He dropped everything into StockLights.com and in the end, he was sunk.

Among the many flaws in Steve's approach was that he allowed himself to get too comfortable with his prospective investing tool. The best thing that he could have done would have been to first assess his comfort level and then evaluate the logistics of the situation that he allowed himself to fall into.

Assessing comfort level is fairly easy. The first step is to determine how many hours of free time you have in a given week. Next, figure out what percentage of those hours you can reasonably spend on managing your portfolio—without detriment to your family or work-life, of course.

Finally, determine your tolerance for loss. Every investor, no matter how well informed, sees a lag in the performance of his or her portfolio once in a while. If you hope to navigate the passage of self-driven investing, you must first reconcile yourself to the fact that you are going to see some setbacks and that in the end, you will have only yourself to blame.

Seeking out reliable sources of information seems like such an elementary concept when it comes to thinking about your investment strategy. It is amazing to see how little research people do for the moves they intend to make. There is no shortage of self-proclaimed experts willing to pontificate on their tips and tricks via the Internet, print media, radio, and television (at all hours of the day and night, no less). Just because they speak loudly or can turn a clever phrase does not mean that they have any idea what they are talking about.

Remember, if somebody is willing to offer an "insider's tip," your first question should be: "Where does his or her motivation come from?" If the many thousands of people reading the column or tuning into the program each day are receiving the same sure-fire tip, at what point does it water down the strategy so much that it becomes useless anyway?

The final note on the subject has already been made. You cannot expect to win for the long-term in the markets without a carefully calculated, well-balanced plan of action. You should not put too much stock in one charting program, just as you should not put too much emphasis in a single news source.

The market and the philosophies that come with it are so incredibly vast that it seems fairly ridiculous to suggest that anyone could find a specific path to its understanding or mastery. Without information drawn from multiple reliable sources and in multiple forms, it is almost impossible to get a clear enough picture of the whole to make sound decisions.

For sure, not every investor is the same. Indeed there are people who have used systems similar to the StockLights.com program to reach some measure of success. It does, in fact, have the potential to be a valuable *supplement* to a sound investment plan. It is just hard to believe in an effective long-term tool that insists that you put all of your eggs in one basket. Instead, you should peruse the many tools that have been listed in this chapter, pick one of each set, and adjust their ranges of information and services to best suit your needs.

The Disciplined Investor's Toolbox

Online and Print News
With the benefits and drawbacks of some of the "easy" stock selection programs, we can dive into the true foundation of the balanced plan. Information is simply key in the quest for knowledge. In order to keep you well informed, the most important task is choosing reliable and trustworthy news sources.

The Daily Read: Investor's Business Daily
Why it is necessary: If you hope to be a well-informed and therefore successful investor, you absolutely need to stay up to date with market news. *Investor's Business Daily* focuses entirely on this topic. It also has an excellent online version packed with many value-added services. The bottom line…it is an essential read.

What it offers: Investment tips, stock lists, daily analysis, newsletters, economics, webcasts, a host of valuable investing tools, a learning center, and the best, most unflinchingly honest market news anywhere. All of these are in the pages of the www.investors.com website as well as the print edition of *IBD*.

Profile of a typical user: IBD is a daily paper offering an excellent source of market news for the investor. It is probably more appropriate for the longer-term investor rather than someone who is actively trading. IBD is most appropriately suited for those who want to understand the markets, and why and how they are moving. The daily stock ratings and rankings are also very highly regarded.

Options: The basic sections of the IBD website offer a great deal of information absolutely free. If you are looking to save money, you may be able to receive the majority of the information you need online, rather than from the print edition. You can also access the entire version of *IBD* online if you purchase an e-subscription.

If you want your news in full and do not want to wait until the next business day (if your *IBD* info would best serve you *before* the markets open or close), you should consider signing up for the e-package. If you are more of a traditionalist, daily print versions can be delivered directly to your door early each business day. If you would prefer to research and read only one day a week, *IBD* also offers a "Monday special" package wherein you receive only one paper per week.

Weekend Reading: *Barron's*

Why it is necessary: If you are an avid trader or a self-driven investor, you already know that just because it is the weekend, your job is not over. If a daily news source is important to keep you up to date on market movement, a good weekend read is essential to keep you in the know when it comes to market trends and the bigger picture. There is no better way to get a sense of where the markets are going than by reading a kind of week- or month-in-review piece like those that are offered in *Barron's*.

What it offers: In-depth articles, featured business and investor profiles, interviews, opinion pieces, commentary, and specific market-related themes can be found in the pages of *Barron's* magazine. Its analysis of the market's impact on daily life and future trends is second to none. Catering to the financial advisor, businessperson, self-driven investor, and casual consumer alike, its articles comprehensively cover the market's influence on key topics of the week such as corporate shifts, political influences, and investment strategies. As an added bonus, it also offers a incredibly extensive listing of economic indicators and weekly stock results.

Profile of a typical reader: Anyone interested in the markets and their movement can find something valuable to read about within *Barron's* pages. However, it qualifies as an *essential* read only for the passionate investor. Some of the topics are advanced and may be beyond the needs of the novice investor.

Options: The print version of the magazine can be purchased with an annual, quarterly, or even monthly subscription. Subscribers can also get the e-version for a nominal additional fee. Both versions are quite good and well worth the price.

Final Word on Barron's: The greatest thing about this magazine is that it seems to be completely unbiased. As mentioned, some publications of this type provide good information; Barron's is fresh and original. Often this periodical will be the first to break a story and is usually right on the mark. If you are looking for weekend news and advice without an agenda, look no further than *Barron's*.

Sunday reading: The *Wall Street Journal* is considered the veritable bible of money management matters. The problem is that it has so much in-depth information that it may be difficult to filter out only the information you need. This might seem like a travesty to some of the more traditional thinkers in the crowd. It is not that the *WSJ* is a bad paper; the truth is it is excellent. One problem with it, though, is that it has three parts, only one of which is specifically dedicated to the markets. While all of the material is superb, some may not be considered required reading. This should be considered a catch-up to be savored on weekends. It will help to fill in, and compliment many of the areas that are not covered in either *IBD* or *Barron's*.

Top Read: *How to Make Money in Stocks: A Winning System in Good Times or Bad* by William O'Neil.

Why it is necessary: For the sake of clarity and thoroughness, sitting down with a good book before beginning to craft an approach to investing should be considered a priority. While magazines and (sometimes) newspapers rarely have shortages of advice about how to invest, their opinions cannot touch the wisdom contained within a good book on the subject. Of course, the word "good" is the operative word here.

In short, this particular book *is* a good one. First of all, it is a wonderfully easy read that provides a basic look at investment strategies and time-tested market indicators. It also represents a no-emotion, no-nonsense, level-headed approach to investing. If a primer is what you need before beginning to invest, then look no further than this classic by William O'Neil.

What it offers: The strategy that this book offers is one of sensibility. As a *Disciplined Investor*, the terms "market capitalization," "daily indexes," and "quarterly earnings" are hopefully not new to you. That is precisely the beauty of this book. It does not try to sell you on gimmicks, it simply provides a proven strategy that employs the use of many of the most common market tools available to an investor.

O'Neil lays out his strategies through extensive examples. Individual stock studies for which some of the data employed stretch back for several decades and appear throughout his chapters. The author uses these studies to shed light on matters such as how to identify a healthy stock, when to cut and run, and how to get out before your investment starts to decline.

Profile of a typical reader: This book would best serve those investors who are just beginning to take their investment matters into their own hands. While people who have been investing for a long time may find the material a little basic, *simplicity*, rather than hyped-up, flashy strategies, is exactly what *The Disciplined Investor* should be looking for.

Final Word on How to Make Money In Stocks: For one, this book was written by the man who went on to create *Investor's Business Daily*. Also, it is a relatively quick read. Most readers will not have any trouble getting through it in a day or two. If limiting losses is one of your goals, you would do well to add this book to your library and its strategies to your financial approach.

Online Personal Finance Services

If you are looking for one-stop shopping for all your personal finance needs, it would be wise to sign up for an online personal finance service (OPFS). While there are many of these services available, only a few of them meet the standards of *The Disciplined Investor*. The following providers are presented in the order of preference.

MSN Money

Why it is necessary: As mentioned, every good investment strategy must be balanced. With that in mind, it is unmistakably apparent that this service is the *essential* foundation to that balanced strategy. Reliable news? Check. Professional-grade tracking tools? Check. Sensible layout? Check. Seamless integration with other applications? Check. Valuable vendor alliances? Check. Security? Check. If you hope to gain an advantage in the markets as well as manage your money effectively, this should be the website in which you spend the majority of your time. *MSN Money* is the definition of a comprehensive online tool.

What it offers: It offers unbelievably sophisticated banking and investing services, and easy-to-use money tracking tools. There are also earnings calculators, planning strategies, and worksheets for retirement. It has a wide range of tools for savings and family, insurance management, estate planning, and tax preparation. In addition, you will find comprehensive research on stocks and funds that includes ratings, charts, and screening systems. It really is a remarkable website. It can be said that not all of these services are "industry best" in their respective categories. Even so you really cannot beat the convenience on the whole.

Profile of a typical user: This is for smart, savvy investors who want to take greater control of their own money but do not want to spend a lot time surfing the Internet. People who enjoy this service tend to point to its user-friendly, cost-effective, and all-encompassing approach to money management.

Options: In researching this book, online and print media were scoured in search of the best value. Without question, this is it. Nothing on the Internet or in print offers so much for so little. Generally there is no cost for this beyond the requirement of providing your email and personal information to Microsoft.

Final Word on MSN Money: Fortunately for the invest-now-and-ask-questions-later kind of consumer, *MSN Money* has gone and gathered all of the essential tools in one place. This is a way to get your news, chart your earnings, track your stocks, plan your retirement, manage your personal bank and credit accounts, and even file your taxes, all on one site. What is more, you can do all of this without being subjected to up-selling or overly obtrusive advertising. It all seems too good to be true, yet it is not. If there were the option of only choosing one of the recommended tools listed, it would have to be this one.

Briefing.com

What it offers: This truly objective resource represents an exceptionally wide range of products and services. Among them are instant market alerts, briefings (hence the name), updates, advice, analysis, and tips.

Where it falls short: For one thing, it carries three distinctive levels of service, all of which carry their own separate fees. You must be wary of this whenever you search for a provider of any kind. For example, *Briefing.com's* lowest service pack only offers market updates every half hour. To get live, to-the-second stock information, you have to pay for the third tier (the priciest package).

Profile of a typical user: The experienced investor would be more apt to use this site. With the highest service pack, it is easy for the minute-to-minute trader to track and manage an average portfolio.

Options: With the basic subscription, you get a stripped-down version of market analysis, calendars, stock analysis, perspectives, tools, and email services and you pay nothing.

For the Platinum Pack—the mid-range solution, you receive live trading reports, live headlines, daily trading ideas, watch list and page alert emails, live coverage of bond markets, and in-depth Federal Reserve and economic analysis. This is available for a monthly fee.

For the Trader Pack—the highest level, you get everything included in the Platinum Pack plus technical trading recommendations with entry/exit points, breakout alerts, live information from trading desks, and candid opinions on intra-day events that combine trading instincts with funda-mental and technical analysis. Additionally, you have access to "under the radar" investment trading ideas. This is a more expensive option and is more appropriate for the profes-sional trader.

Final Word on Briefing.com: The services offered by this company certainly do represent a great bang for the buck for news, in-depth strategies, and alerts. You get what you pay for on *Briefing.com*, and what you pay for is exceptional quality. The trouble is that there is a cost and the top package is cer-tainly not cheap. Almost everything offered through this site is available for free on the *MSN Money* site. In fact, some of the news on *MSN Money* is provided by *Briefing.com*.

Dismal.com

What it offers: High quality and a wide range of market cover-age. This tool seems to be aimed at the globally conscious investor, having segregated the major markets of each conti-nent. With this service, you will receive many of the same benefits offered by *Briefing.com*. It provides a broad, top-down overview of the world and the pulse of its economy. First and foremost, this is an economic reporting and commentary site.

Where it falls short: Again, much of the meat of this serv-ice is found in the paid subscription level. To be sure, there is a good amount of information to be found on the basic site. There is a subscription price for what they call "editions" (corners of the globe covered by their market research). The editions include Asia/Pacific, Europe, Latin America, the U.S., and Canada, and each comes with its own separate, additional fee.

Profile of a typical user: This service is best employed by an investor who utilizes a top-down approach to investment research and strategy. Typically, this person is looking for a (relatively) inexpensive method of researching the global markets. Do not, however, confuse inexpensive with a lack of quality. This site offers a tremendous amount of idea-generating tools and commentary.

Options: Some of the site is free. Otherwise the cost depends on the number of editions you want. Each has its own fee and is available on a monthly or annual basis.

Final Word on Dismal.com: If you are a global thinker, you really cannot beat Dismal.com. It is highly recommended by both *Forbes* and *Barron's*, so you know you are getting quality when you sign up for this service. In addition, it is an adjunct site to Economy.com, one of the best of breed for economic research.

Web- and Desktop-Based Informational Tools

It has been shown that thorough research is at the core of any well-designed investment plan. Yet who says it has to be time-consuming and mentally draining? Rather than spending half of your day searching for statistics and trends, why not simply download them or sign up for a piece of software that does all the searching and compiling for you?

StockCharts.com
What it offers: This is essentially an online tool for creating and researching charts. The service is quite valuable and will help provide you with an array of technical analysis tools. In fact, some of the companies and sites listed previously utilize charts created by *StockCharts.com* for their sites. This company offers everything

from chart tracking and creation tools to educational materials that include anything you could ever want to know about reading or building an effective chart. They also employ an impressive and reliable support structure headed by the company's guru, John Murphy. They even offer an informative newsletter.

Profile of a typical user: Anyone who feels that an accurate chart may help him or her visualize the most appropriate strategies for investing.

Options: This tool is also divided into various subscription levels. There is a pretty good cross-section of charts and charting services available for free, but a user who wants all the bells and whistles will have to pay a modest subscription fee. There are also advanced packages that include additional charting and analysis.

Final Word on StockCharts.com: Much of the site is free. If you choose to subscribe, you will notice that for what you pay, you really get a lot. This product is probably best suited for those who wish to gain an advantage from having a sophisticated charting tool. For the most part, the charts and the technical analysis features are the best out there. Even so, with all of the online materials that are offered free, this may represent an avoidable expense.

MarketBrowser.com

What it offers: This is an exceptionally flashy and user-friendly tool that allows you to track investments at a glance via a whole range of simultaneously running charts and graphs. It provides one-click access to more detailed information on a stock. In its most expanded view, this product reveals a range of colorful charts that are dynamically updated and fill your entire computer screen. Other views provide a less-intrusive look and take up less desktop real estate. Using this as a hub to organize your investments will prove beneficial. The program has an unbelievable depth of options built right in.

Profile of a typical user: Anyone who is looking for a good charting and quoting service for a low cost.

Cost: Free.

Final Word on MarketBrowser: This is an excellent point-and-click service that could well serve as the hub to track your investment plan. It is most beneficial for those who are visually inclined, however, as its overall look and feel can be a bit intense and chart-heavy. Be aware that there is no cost for this service, and as such the quotes are delayed 20 minutes.

Self-Directed Brokerage Firms

The following companies offer many essential services for the true do-it-yourselfer. Each has its own benefits and drawbacks, though, so it is important to read as much as you can on the backgrounds of each company before you take the plunge and use them to invest.

When researching an online brokerage firm, be sure to read between the lines about their products, services and general account terms. Remember, what you see is not always what you get.

Charles Schwab
What it offers: In addition to the obvious "for-fee" trading services and passive financial advice that you might find at any of these self-directed brokerage firms, Schwab offers a specialized

trading platform—CyberTrader. This software program is one of the best available for the day trader. This incredibly advanced platform presents a substantial amount of information and is a powerhouse for serious day traders.

Profile of a typical user: A serious trader, a day trader, or anyone who wants to have a deeper sense of control over his or her own investing. It is a good idea to have an advanced understanding of trading and the Level II markets. It is also a prerequisite to understand advanced charting and the order entry process.

Options: Trading will have costs associated with each transaction depending on the amount of activity and the size of the trade. The CyberTrader software may also have fees depending on your personal trading profile.

Of course, there may be other fees associated with getting advice, trading, asset custody, and so on. Frankly there are too many to list here, though they are all sensible and fully disclosed. To view a comprehensive list of fees, visit www.schwab.com and navigate to the commissions and fees area.

Final Word on Schwab: In addition to its excellent trading software and reputation for superior customer service, Schwab offers a huge inventory of mutual funds. Some may have transaction fees and some may not. The company also has more service centers around the country than any of the other firms that fall under this category. For most individuals looking to have a healthy blend of service with a reasonable fee structure, this company probably warrants the most consideration.

Other Firms (Fidelity, E*TRADE, TD Ameritrade, etc.)

What they offer: There are, of course, subtle nuances to each of these companies, but all offer generally similar services. They also offer up-to-date information pertaining to your brokerage account, are very secure, and provide ample research on stocks and mutual fund investments along with trading and money management advice.

Where they fall short: For the most part, the charting services, research, and news provided by these companies is average at best. Also, their banking services could use a little work. In some cases, the customer service leaves a lot to be desired. Most of the differences lie in the fact that each of us has our own unique wants and needs. Some like chocolate, some vanilla. That does not mean that one is necessarily better than the other.

Profile of a typical user: This person is interested in tools that provide accurate account information but less interested in the research. These are all suitable companies for most investors and as noted, it really comes down to a matter of personal preference.

Options: The fee structure, in almost all cases, is very similar to that of Schwab. Each company will have an area of specialty that will put it ahead of the other for that service. Overall, there is not much criticism that can be directed toward any of these fine firms.

Final Word on the others: Even if you put the "independent" in "independent investor," it is important to consider employing a company such as one of those listed in this section to help centrally manage your portfolio. However, tools and services provided by all of these companies are by no means considered replacements for the ones provided by companies such as *StockCharts*. Even so, they are all excellent additions for most investors.

Money-Management Software

While this portion of the balanced plan may be on its way out (at least in the out-of-the-box sense of the word), a few money-management tools should be considered. They may not provide the best advice to help you plan your investment approach, but they are certainly effective when it comes to organizing your holdings.

There are only two such software programs that dominate the industry, and they are quite similar. A quick discussion of each will be presented here.

Around 1995, a few companies began to work on the idea of creating account aggregation software that would help to consolidate a person's financial accounts. Two companies, Quicken and Microsoft, believed this kind of software would promote changes as dramatic as the day man put down his slide-rule and picked up a calculator. Today, both companies have programs and sites that are excellent to help consolidate your finances. They are completely configurable and user-friendly, and are quite useful when it comes to integrating the numbers on your computer with the numbers provided by your bank, credit card company, or brokerage.

Since they are so exceptional for managing a virtual bank account, it should come as a surprise that they not at that same level when used for investment accounts. They have the capability of syncing with online brokerage firms, but tend to come up short in the actual delivery. With their lack of real time function and without accurate charting features, they both represent a rich set of possibilities that falls rather flat. In any case, their only real benefit is the enhanced security over the alternative of having several online accounts with differing passcodes and usernames. It is important to stress that the Internet is not the insecure environment that it was only a few years ago.

Also, anyone who gets nervous about typing his account information into a website should probably consider the fact that they quite regularly, willingly, and happily hand their credit cards over to waiters, hotel clerks, and the like. Who knows what an unscrupulous person may do with that kind of opportunity?

Conclusion

As an investor, it is possible to do all the research in the world and create the most detailed projections imaginable about the future. You may also be talented at making investment decisions, and may be very successful at sifting through all of the over-hyped advice available to you. Even so, you may still find yourself overworked and your portfolio underperforming. It is *The Disciplined Investor* who understands the reasons for this and, as such, takes all the steps necessary to create the most balanced plan of action possible.

The tools listed herein are designed with the self-driven investor in mind. The good news is that if you were so inclined, you could manage your own portfolio for a relatively low price. Even if you do not own a computer and must start entirely from scratch, you can still be up and running and managing your own assets with start-up costs under $1,000.

Although the material presented in this chapter may seem a bit overwhelming, each of the tools mentioned can help to enhance and simplify the process of managing a portfolio. Realize that no matter how efficient you are at it, money management is still a time-consuming and difficult endeavor.

Remember, finding success on your own may be an incredibly liberating and fulfilling achievement, but the central goal to all of this is to make money efficiently and protect it well.

It is true that making money is the most important thing when investing, but it is also true that the second most important thing is balancing that with an appropriate comfort level. If it becomes too much to handle, *The Disciplined Investor* must be able to identify the need for help and accept advice. In response to that fact, the next chapter covers everything from guarding your assets to picking the proper advisor.

Chapter 9

Implementing the Plan

Now that you are well on your way to understanding how to best use the tools for choosing an investment, how do you decide which asset classes will provide the best return with the least risks? This question needs to be answered on an ongoing basis. If the task becomes overwhelming you may want to consider hiring a qualified advisor to assist with many of the important day-to-day decisions. You can hire outside help for your entire portfolio or simply to get assistance with the overall asset allocation model.

You need a plan, a roadmap, and directions. Otherwise, you may find yourself chasing your tail. Here is a common story that helps to illustrate this key point:

A man from North Dakota was headed to Montana for a three-week ice-fishing trip. En route, a massive snowstorm blew in, reducing the drive to a crawling pace. Undeterred, the man kept on driving since he did not want to miss this great fishing opportunity.

In time, his perseverance paid off, and he saw a snowplow churning up ahead. In a few moments, he was behind the plow—and driving on concrete again for the first time in hours. He was thrilled to be on-track once again.

For the next 20 minutes or so, the man followed the snow-plow, happy to have finally caught a break in his star-crossed journey. His happiness was short-lived, however, because after a few more minutes he watched as the plow operator came to a stop, cut off his engine, and began slowly trudging his way back toward him. In a moment, the plow operator was beside the man's car, rapping on the glass with his gloved knuckle.

As the window opened, the plow operator began to speak. "Where you headed, buddy?" he asked.

"Montana," said the man as he wondered what this was all about.

"Montana? That's a long way from here. Especially in this storm."

"Yep. Good thing I've got you paving the way, huh?"

The plow operator politely smirked and then laughed out loud. When he finally gained his composure, he began to speak again. "Well, sir, you're gonna have a tough time getting there if you plan to keep following me," he said.

"Oh yeah? Why's that?" the man asked with curiosity.

"Look around you, buddy. I'm plowing a parking lot."

It might seem slightly absurd, but this story is perfect for highlighting the importance of having an investment plan with a system of checks and balances to ensure you stay on course. Even if you have learned everything you will ever need to know about how to analyze and create a strategy for investing, your portfolio may still take a dive without proper management.

Fortunately, the industry has created both a term and a strategy to help the average investor avoid blindly following plows. It is known as **asset allocation**. 📖

📖 ASSET ALLOCATION
The way in which an investment portfolio is divided among different kinds of assets, such as stocks, bonds, real estate, or cash equivalents. By investing in different kinds of assets, an investor can balance growth potential and risk. It is also a process that provides ongoing rebalancing of portfolio positions to ensure it remains properly diversified.

The first thing to know when considering the prospect of asset allocation is that, as do most things related to investing, it comes in many forms. The simplest concept to grasp is that in order to avoid incredible downside risk, you have to diversify. As a *Disciplined Investor*, you cannot put all your eggs in one basket and expect your portfolio to perform consistently.

To illustrate, here is the simple (and pretty flowery) metaphor:

Recall that in Chapter 5 it was suggested that a portfolio should look and act like a flower garden. Comparing your investments to a flower garden may seem strange, but the idea is to have a portfolio stand up to the test of time and its changing seasons. You will want to have the gorgeous colors and you will also need a good mix of perennials. Your garden (portfolio) should include varieties (sectors) that need direct sun along with those that grow better in the shade. For good measure, add some evergreens (cash equivalents), as they will stay in bloom during even the harshest months.

You need to strongly consider the climate of where your garden is growing, similar to the economic climate for your portfolio. Your portfolio needs to be able to stand up to the harsh winters seen as the sporadic storms of the economy.

It is possible to go as far as building a portfolio that is almost completely risk-free, but the tradeoff comes with the loss of upside potential. Risk-free portfolios are entirely predictable. They are not going to lose much money, but they are probably not going to gain much, either. If you want that upside, you have to be willing to balance it against some measure of risk.

During the early portion of the last century, Benjamin Graham suggested that a perfectly diversified portfolio carried a position in stocks, bonds, cash, and real estate. That seems clear-cut enough. The statement certainly outlines the basis for a balanced plan, although that simple definition is not enough anymore. Markets are more complicated in our ever-expanding and ever-volatile investment environment.

For example, bonds are not what they used to be. What had been a fairly straightforward topic can now be broken down into complicated categories that sometimes carry non-intuitive names. When sizing up a bond, it is important to know more than if it is simply a municipal, corporate, or government bond. You have to know what each category means, too. Furthermore, each of those categories can be segregated into subcategories such as maturity, rating, pre-refunding, tax qualification, and so on.

The modern significance of asset allocation came from the minds of three academics named Brinson, Hood, and Beebower (BHB). In the late 1980s, they determined that somewhere between 90 and 93.6 percent of all portfolio returns could be explained by the chosen mix of assets. The study was titled, "Determinants of Portfolio Performance." Essentially, this meant that allocation decisions, rather than specific investment decisions, dictated portfolio performance.

Of course, as with everything in this free-world economy, there are polar opposite viewpoints to point out. At that time, economic scholars like Ibbotson and Kaplan essentially backed the BHB claims. They went on further to say that these studies demonstrated asset allocation's responsibility for 100 percent of returns over time, 90 percent of variability of returns over time, and 40 percent of variability of returns from investment manager to investment manager.

Of course, it probably did not hurt that Ibbotson's company was also marketing a complex and expensive software package that aided advisors with the application of asset allocation theories based on the BHB study.

Not long after, there was a ground-breaking follow-up study by William Jahnke which suggested that asset allocation was only a viable measure of success in the absence of traditional active trading and security selection. Jahnke believed that strategies like market timing and researched stock selection were just as important to a portfolio's performance as allocating assets.

In fact, in the February 1997 edition of the *Journal of Financial Planning*, Jahnke wrote a controversial article entitled "The Asset Allocation Hoax" contradicting the BHB study. He clearly and rather convincingly wrote that "While most investors agree that explaining the range of returns over their investment horizon is more important than explaining the fluctuations of quarterly returns, short-term volatility of returns is also important. However, the study misrepresents the relative importance asset allocation policy has on portfolio volatility when Brinson, Hood and Beebower observe that asset allocation policy explains 93.6 percent of the variation in quarterly portfolio returns. They define variation as the variance of quarterly returns. In fact, the most appropriate measure is the standard deviation of quarterly returns, which operates in the same units of measurement as return. That is why portfolio risk is reported in terms of standard deviation, not variance."

He went on further to suggest, "While the BHB study observes that asset allocation policy explains 93.6 percent of the variance of quarterly portfolio returns, when using the more appropriate standard deviation asset allocation policy explains only 79 percent of the variation of quarterly returns. Though still a big number, it does not appear to be as conclusive as the reported 93.6 percent." That was the final nail in the study's coffin.

The excitement around what was thought to be a revolutionary breakthrough was subdued. Regular talk about the asset allocation process and the more common use of the mean variance optimization strategy diminished. The timing was rather coincidental to the huge gains in the market toward the end of the millennium. During that time, there was no pressing need for a sophisticated strategy to help make money beyond throwing a few darts at a newspaper's business section.

What remained was the principal that asset allocation of a portfolio could be quantified using statistics. The fine technique of employing historical measures together with forward predictions can help investors mathematically optimize portfolios in order to reduce their risk.

It is a complicated matter, yes, but there are really only three core terms that you need to know before considering a strategy based on the complex and more sophisticated asset allocation process. They are: <u>**mean variance optimization,**</u> 📖 <u>**the efficient frontier**</u> 📖 and <u>**semi-variance.**</u> 📖

📖   MEAN VARIANCE OPTIMIZATION (MVO)
A calculated ratio that measures the amount of risk an investor is willing to take in comparison to the anticipated level of return. This methodology takes a look at historical economic environments and tries to emulate them, projecting the expected return into the future.

📖   THE EFFICIENT FRONTIER (EF)
This term is related to MVO in the sense that it is the ultimate goal of that calculation to find the greatest risk/reward ratio. The Efficient Frontier refers to the point of a portfolio's greatest competence. Once optimized, an investor and an advisor can sit down and determine which blend of foreign, domestic, and bond investments is necessary to best emulate the Efficient Frontier. If a portfolio passes a certain point on the risk/reward scale, there is no further benefit that can be realized by changing the allocation. The Efficient Frontier shows the "sweet spot" related to risk and reward.

📖 SEMI-VARIANCE (SV)

This term refers to how much downside risk can be associated with a given portfolio. It is a benchmark for risk in the same way that the EF is a benchmark for performance. The term enjoyed great popularity following the downturn that culminated in the spring of 2000. At that time almost everybody, regardless of how well diversified their portfolios were, took a significant beating because of the market correction. Essentially, if you stayed the course, you got hurt. If you tried to reallocate your assets, you had a hard time due to the complete lack of relatable historical evidence to base the current situation upon. There was nowhere to hide, and even portfolios created with the finest allocation systems were vulnerable to the market's rage.

With all of that in mind, it is easy to see that asset allocation is more than a complicated process. It would be impossible to get into all the tools and methodologies available to the average investor without a significant lesson on statistics and market theory. Rather, here is a quick fix for how to size up your risk needs. In this case, stocks (an investment on the higher end of the risk spectrum) will be used as the measure.

While it may be overly simplistic, here is a start: to assess your percentage of risk tolerance, consider your age against the backdrop of 100 years. If you are 60, assessing the kind of risk you should be willing to take is as simple as subtracting 60 from 100. Therefore, you should have a portfolio that includes 40 percent stocks. If you are 50, it is 50 percent, and so on.

This simple calculation is certainly not the only thing you will need in order to craft a sensible asset allocation plan, but again, it will at least get you started. Then, you will know just how much risk and stability you will need in order to maximize your ability to continue making money after retirement and, at the same time, avoid the withering of your nest egg due to cost of living increases.

What Asset Allocation Is and Is Not

First of all, the task does not simply involve buying three different mutual funds. Mutual funds, by their nature, are an excellent way to avoid putting all your eggs in one basket. That does not translate to the idea that you can just pick a few and be done with it.

For example, an investor who purchases mutual funds such as the Vanguard Index 500, the Wilshire Index 5000, and the American Funds Fundamental Investors may believe that his or her portfolio has a diverse foundation. Without doing the research, though, the investor will have grossly overlapped investments since many of the stocks that these funds hold are the same.

Basically, a person investing this way is buying many of the same stocks, only doing it through three different avenues without diversifying.

A better solution would be to buy a small cap fund, a mid cap fund, a large cap fund, an international fund, and possibly even a sector fund like health care, gold, oil, or natural resources.

Remember that asset allocation is not a quantifiable science, even if you use the most complex optimization software. Any website or advertisement that claims to have developed a tool that can comprehensively assess your asset allocation needs is a bit too enthusiastic. This is because allocating assets is a matter of reducing risk, and risk is not always a black and white issue. There are just too many human biases and data-mining scenarios, which a piece of software cannot accurately predict. Asset allocation, therefore, should be considered more of an art form.

Working With an Advisor

Protecting your assets from all the potential pitfalls can be a rather trying matter. For many people, enjoying money is much more rewarding than constantly searching for ways to improve the bottom line. For others, it may make better financial or personal sense to focus daily attention on their career, their family, or retirement, and let a paid professional handle the kind of painstaking research it takes to maintain a profitable portfolio.

Fortunately, for the many people out there who do not like the idea of braving the waters alone, there is an entire fleet of financial professionals willing to help. The degree and quality of that advice varies greatly, and as this book has stressed again and again, it is important to do your homework.

Financial professionals come from many different backgrounds, biases, skill sets, and influences, and have varied levels of experience. Therefore is it imperative to assess the kind of investment strategies you are looking for as well as the kind of person you would like to work with. It is critical that you take the time to size up the benefits and drawbacks of dealing with a particular financial advisor as if you are looking to buy and test-drive a car.

During your evaluation, there are a few easily recognizable key indicators that *The Disciplined Investor* must pay attention to. The following two segments conveniently lump them into two categories: what to avoid and what to look for.

Choosing an Advisor: What You Should Know
At the grocery store, most people comparison shop. They are not likely to buy a $2.00 can of corn from one reputable brand when another equally reputable name is selling for $1.50. Unless, of course, you are dealing with a canned corn connoisseur. In that case the discerning consumer would more likely buy the $5.00 can that was imported from Europe.

Choosing an advisor is a similar process and carries many of the same potential influences. Know this: when looking for an advisor, you usually get what you pay for.

Getting what you pay for, in this case, has a rather complicated connotation, especially considering that you are not just dealing with varying price tags. This time you are also dealing with varying pricing *structures*. It is true that highly regarded, experienced advisors tend to charge more than lesser known or inexperienced advisors. It is also true that the method of payment tends to complicate things. Financial advisors earn their income by charging their clients in one of the following manners:

- Pay-per-trade
- Fee-only
- Fee-based
- Commission-based

Pay-Per-Trade: This is a term that refers to any advisory practice that charges a rate for the simple act of trading a stock or other investment. The term "pay-per-trade" actually refers to the kind of online, self-directed investment approach covered in Chapter 8. Some companies employ advisors who may receive a base salary. In addition, bonuses may be based on the many thousands of flat-rate trading fees that the company earns every day from the clients that use their services. For the most part, this type of advisor is considered a "broker" and merely assists with your trades rather than providing advice.

Fee-Only: This term refers to the type of advisor that charges a standard hourly fee, a flat fee, or a percentage fee for his or her advice. Think of the way in which one pays a lawyer or psychiatrist. This sort of pay structure may also come with an annual fee associated with the types of investments that you and your advisor agree on. Most often, you will pay a percentage of the assets managed for ongoing advice and support beyond the initial consultation.

Fee-Based: This is probably the loosest term in the entire group. Fee-based advisors may charge a flat hourly rate plus a fee for managing your portfolio. In addition, investments purchased may pay a commission to the advisor. The degree of those commissions varies greatly between advisors and some firms will actually work in a manner closer to the category of fee-only than others. With this arrangement, clients will have the broadest range of investment options available to them.

Commission-Based: Anyone who has ever gone into a shoe store or car dealership knows that salespeople who live exclusively off of commissions are nothing short of relentless when it comes to their advice on products or services they represent. If they do not get you to "pull out the old checkbook" they do not make any money. It is essentially the same with commission-based advisors, who are paid only when you implement suggestions that they make on stocks, loaded mutual funds, insurance, or annuity products.

In summary, you can determine what to avoid in an advisor by following a few basic rules. The first is that while the online, self-directed advisory firms may be great for those who wish to maintain some degree of control over their own portfolios, when it comes time to offer expert advice, they tend to fall short. Basically, it is pretty easy to figure out that the advisors working for one of these services (with no commission, a base salary, and little motivation to perform well for the client) may not exactly be the "cream of the crop."

The second point is that when dealing with a fee-only advisor (specifically those that charge by the hour) you may find yourself paying for some services that you do not really need. Look at an interior decorator analogy: it may happen that your new decorator takes a look at your entire home and tells you that everything is perfect and no changes are needed. More probable though, he or she will suggest all of the things that need to be updated and improved. Of course this service will be provided for an hourly fee. Even with that analogy in mind, the fee-only advisor is still an excellent choice if you are looking for ongoing investment management.

Then there are advisors that are primarily commission-based. Imagine for a moment that you are in a mall shopping for shoes. You walk into a well-stocked retail establishment and find that it *only* sells brown shoes. The pleasant salesman walks over and asks if you need help. Let's agree that you are most assuredly not going to walk out of there with a brand new pair of black shoes. No matter how badly you may want a black pair, the benefits and beauty of the brown shoes will be extolled.

Now, with that in mind, think about the commission-based planner. If you are working with an advisor whose income is based on the commissions from selling specific investments, how can you ever be certain that what you are buying is not a membership at the country club for that advisor?

At what point does adding a mutual fund to the portfolio or jumping on a stock become an action that is less in your interest and more in theirs?

By process of elimination, the best pick out of the group is the fee-based advisor. Typically, these advisors employ a nice blend of all the fee structures. Basically, you will be able to choose which pay structure is best suited for you *and* the advisor. This gives you the greatest flexibility and control.

Apart from the fee structure, there are additional factors to consider when determining the best advisor for your unique situation.

Choosing an Advisor: What to Look For

Before deciding which specific advisor to hire, the best approach would be to assess what kind of investor you are. That may not seem like the easiest task at first. Fortunately, there have been several studies done over the past few decades that have focused squarely on the range of investor styles. When it comes to managing assets, studies show that most people can be divided into three groups:

- Do-it-yourselfers
- Collaborators
- Outsourcers

Do-It-Yourselfers: These investors are likely to gain the most from carefully reading Chapter 8. They have a propensity toward absolute control over a portfolio's destiny. The problem with trying to control your destiny is that it does not always go as planned. Good or bad, the pure do-it-yourselfers are rather unlikely to ever seek the aid of a financial advisor of any kind. If they do, it is likely that the relationship will be short-lived.

Collaborators: These investors prefer to maintain some sense of control, but recognize that the process of managing a portfolio is something that they cannot do on their own. They tend to view the advisor-advisee relationship in much the same manner as a partnership. They like to delegate responsibility rather than handling it on their own. This is the classical definition of a "team effort." Both parties are working with a common goal, synergistically.

Outsourcers: This group of investors would rather play golf or do almost anything other than have the "chained-to-the-desk" feeling that comes with watching the stock-ticker all day. They enjoy the prospect of being able to hand their financial matters over to an experienced and trusted advisor. Their plan is to let the advisor do the work and then simply forget about it for a while. Of course, these are the same people who can get "burned" unless they do a good amount of research before choosing an advisor. If they fail to employ the services of a reputable professional with the proper experience, they may find themselves with poorly constructed financial plans. On top of that, if the advisor is not keeping portfolio performance in line with the investor's goals, the extreme outsourcer will never know if their advisor is staying on course.

In some capacity, it is important to seek counsel of some kind. Bear in mind that old saying: The man who represents himself as an attorney has a fool for a client. Nobody—not even an experienced advisor—has the answers to all of life's (or Wall Street's) questions. Furthermore, almost no one can completely separate their emotions from their own portfolio. This happens to be one of the most important lessons to be learned when dealing with your own money.

That is why advisors have a decided advantage. If they gain or lose $5,000 in a day for your portfolio, they are less likely to lose sleep over it. Of course this is not something to be taken lightly, even with a very large portfolio. Yet the simple fact of the gain or loss is less likely to dictate the advisors' next move. This is what separates the successful investor from the rest of the pack.

In short, the greatest benefit of utilizing an investment advisor, in some capacity, is to gain *objectivity*. Portfolio decisions that are based on logic, rather than emotion, will be much more consistent with your long-term goals.

Take some time to assess what type of investor you are. Once you have a good idea, start to think about whether or not you want to even consider using an advisor. Either way, you now have a good base of knowledge and are on the road to becoming a *Disciplined Investor*.

If you feel that you would like to explore the advisor route, here are a few important points you can use as a check-list in the interview process. These are the main areas to focus on, though they are definitely not the only ones you should ask about. A capable advisor has any number of the following to his or her credit:

- Certified Financial Planner™ (CFP) certification
- Experience
- Independent status
- Full-time status
- State insurance license
- An excellent and well-supported reputation

Not all of these are requirements. For example, if you are only interested in an advisor working with your investments, an insurance license may not be of consequence. On the other hand, a full-time status is non-negotiable. There is no way that this important profession can be moonlighted. If someone tells you that they can help you in their spare time, run fast!

Look once more at the list. CFPs occupy the first position for one good reason: They are committed and hard working enough to pass the rigorous and exhaustive examination process that comes with the territory.

Becoming a CFP certificant is not easy, as evidenced by how relatively few there are in this country. To put this into perspective, it is reported that as of 2007, there are approximately 50,000 Certified Financial Planners as compared to over 500,000 Certified Public Accountants (CPAs). The main benefit to the consumer is that the CFP certification is a sign that shows advisors who are serious, committed and career-minded. Of course there are also several other designations that may help to identify qualified advisors such as ChFC, CLU, PFS, CFA, among others. However, realize that "qualified" does not necessarily mean they are "good."

CFP certificants are usually able to take a broader and more balanced look at your goals, your future, and your investment needs. They are also better equipped to provide you with a wide range of non-investment-related services. The curriculum they study covers the gamut of financial planning matters, which is in sharp contrast to similar certifications that focus more time on insurance sales and marketing.

Expert financial advice is a lot like major league pitching: experience plays a huge role. A rookie is far less likely to construct a time-tested and watertight plan for you than a seasoned veteran. As a rule of thumb, you should seek out an advisor that has *at least* five years of service under his or her belt.

Independent advisors are also better equipped to meet your needs than those who are associated with a big insurance or brokerage firm. This is because advisors who work for one of the big names on Wall Street may be required by the company to sell you many of the products that their company markets.

These are usually termed "proprietary." For example, if the brokerage firm your advisor works with is Worthmore Investments and the fund she recommends is the Worthmore Stock Fund, start asking questions.

Is there a financial incentive or bonus for the recommendation of this investment? How does it stack up against its peers? Are the fees competitive? What are the other options and why are they not being presented?

What if there is a cheaper financial product offered by a competing firm, but you have been pigeon-holed into buying the more expensive one from your advisor's affiliated company? Who is benefiting from this? Basically, an independent advisor is not hindered by a narrow range of products and services. He or she does not try to pound a square peg into a round hole.

At some point in the life of many successful advisors, there comes a time when a great deal of the work can be pawned off on an assistant or rookie partner. The trouble with an advisor who spends more time away from the desk than at it is that he or she may often miss investment opportunities that could have served you quite well.

Choose an advisor who spends at least 8 to 10 hours per day directly serving the needs of their clients, rather than wearing the hat of the firm marketer. Unless there is a staff member or partner that you have agreed to work with in advance, your advisor should be the primary contact for your finances.

Of course, for the administrative matters, the advisor may not be needed, so make sure you develop a good relationship with the office administration and staff. Though you may not think so at first, they are a key component to your long-term success.

A state insurance license means that your advisor deals with more than just market investments—it means that they can provide a whole host of value-added services to help you meet many of the needs that will help protect your money. Most effective asset allocation plans include some kind of insurance. Can your advisor provide that for you?

The final point is the most traditional and the most important. Choosing an advisor, like choosing any product or service, is still essentially a "smell test." It is still a good practice to ask a friend or get a professional recommendation. The process still comes with an awful lot of gut feeling. You can find an advisor who has the world's greatest track record behind them, but if you are not comfortable in their presence, keep looking.

Continue to ask your friends about their advisors. Find out what they like or dislike about them. Then, interview two or three of the best candidates for the job. Hold yourself back from picking the one with the cheapest services because you are most likely to get what you pay for.

Never underestimate the importance of written materials. If a potential advisor has written and published articles, a book, or a newsletter that you can read—something more than a shiny and colorful brochure—at least you can see what areas they have specific knowledge and expertise in. In addition, written materials serve as historical evidence for what an advisor has done in the past. If they have *documented proof* that they bought Google and then stuck with it, that might be a good thing to know.

Chapter 10

Putting It All Together

Now what? You are equipped with all this new wisdom and it is time to take the next step and put everything into action. Throughout this book, many key points have been presented for you to consider when crafting an investment portfolio on your own. Before getting into the heart of the matter, though, it may be prudent to review the central tenets of what has been covered.

You have learned that to have a successful investment strategy you must apply a strict and sturdy sense of discipline. It is easy to be tempted by the get-rich kind of mentality that can sometimes come with market investing. It is essential to stay focused and, where possible, conservative. To that end, assessing your risk tolerance is the first and most important step when constructing a plan for a better future.

You have also learned that emotions must be kept as far away from investment decisions as possible. With the strict application of quantitative investing, you can filter out and navigate through all of the potential biases that line the way to successful investing.

Studying the present while keeping a sharp eye on the past is a smart idea. This will boost your overall success with the application of technical analysis. The markets tend to follow trends that can be fairly well predicted if you are willing to do the research and you have the right data at hand. With a finely honed understanding of history, you may be able to better determine the direction of a market's future.

Fundamental analysis, meanwhile, teaches us that while employing a focus on trends may be a good idea, before investing in a given company it might also behoove any investor to learn everything that he or she can about it. Earnings histories, balance sheets, and product lines, along with details on management structure and staff: all of this essential information is a part of public record and, more often than not, as a package, serves as an excellent economic indicator for any publicly traded stock.

Distant and not-so-distant history has also taught the harsh lesson of the benefit of a well-planned risk management strategy. Look no further than the turn of this century to see how easy it is to get caught up in the rising tides of a charging bull market, only to lose your bottom dollar when the bear finally rears its ugly head once again.

Many have suggested that the best way to avoid this lose-your-shirt kind of scenario is to invest heavily in mutual funds, but again, even the prepackaged, reduced-risk, and increased-stability kinds of investments require a good amount of smart research. As with anything else, not all mutual funds are created equal. Remember: it is important to do your homework.

A valuable lesson learned is that annuities and guaranteed investment contracts, while attractive investment strategies, tend to come in all different shapes and sizes. In order to maximize this kind of investment, it is crucial to understand the many pitfalls and study the fine print in each product.

This book finishes with the topic of choosing an advisor for a good reason. Nobody—not even those intrepid readers who took the time to absorb all the information written in this and other books—has all the answers. The best portfolio is created on the foundation of *diversity*. The best practice for managing a portfolio is based on *collaboration*. Two minds—especially when one of them is able to remove a good part of the emotion from the equation—are better than one.

From the beginning, you have learned the value and importance of sound and thorough analysis. The analytical approach is in fact the best way to separate yourself from the "feelings" (gut or otherwise) that tend to lead to investment decisions that are made with the heart instead of the head.

As with anything in life, you must take heed of the past and study the details of the present if you ever hope to predict the future. Because there are so many indices and trends to take into consideration, you must remain ever-vigilant to the numbers at hand. They have a story to tell and if you hope to beat the markets and make your investments matter, you must listen to and study that story as thoroughly as possible.

In response to uncertainty a great many sound strategies have been devised to help keep your portfolio safe. There are a myriad of security nets at your disposal. It is important to size up the viability of each. Opinions, goals, and fears vary from investor to investor. Before you may begin to build an investment strategy, you must first determine the best path to protect yourself from the random downturns that the economy and the markets are sure to take.

Investment tools are plentiful in today's highly connected marketplace, but the sheer abundance of tools does not equate to quality. If you indeed plan to venture off into the world of investing on your own, be sure to do your homework on the applications that you intend to employ. Not all of them are as accurate or thorough as *The Disciplined Investor* calls for.

No matter how you intend to invest, be sure to protect your investments. If anything has been learned from the sharp decline that followed the turn of this millennium, it should be that the markets are never immune to corrections, even if it seems that "this time will be different." There is no such thing as a sure-fire investment bet. There are no "get-rich-quick" schemes that work. Take the time to protect yourself from such inclinations.

With this book as a guide and tool, you now have an excellent base for evaluating the methods and strategies for developing a winning and balanced financial plan. Do your research and, above all, maintain your discipline, and you will be well on your way to finding success.

NOTES

NOTES

Quick Order Form

Email orders: sales@thedisciplinedinvestor.com
Fax orders: 954-349-1414 (Send this form)
Telephone orders: Call (954)349-0800
                or toll free, (888)964-PLAN (7526).

Postal orders:
HFactor Publishing ATT: TDI Sales
1555 NorthPark Drive #102, Weston, Florida 33326

Please send the following Books, Discs or Reports. I understand that I may return any of them for a full refund—for any reason, no questions asked.

Book Title _____

Please send more FREE information on: (circle all that apply)

Other books Speaking/Seminars Audiobooks Consulting

Name _____
Address _____
City _____State _____ Zip _____
Telephone _____
Email address _____

Shipping: $4 for the first book or disk and $2 for each additional product.

Payment: Check or Credit card (Visa, MasterCard, AMEX)

Card number _____

Name on card _____ Exp. Date___/___

http://www.thedisciplinedinvestor.com